THE

Little Green Book

OF

Absinthe

THE

Little Green Book

OF

Absinthe

AN ESSENTIAL COMPANION
WITH LORE, TRIVIA, AND CLASSIC AND
CONTEMPORARY COCKTAILS

Paul Owens and Paul Nathan

Drink Recipes by Dave Herlong

A PERIGEE BOOK

A PERIGEE BOOK
Published by the Penguin Group
Penguin Group (USA) Inc.
375 Hudson Street, New York, New York 10014, USA
Penguin Group (Canada), 90 Eglinton Avenue East, Suite 700, Toronto, Ontario M4P 2Y3, Canada
(a division of Pearson Penguin Canada Inc.)
Penguin Books Ltd., 80 Strand, London WC2R 0RL, England
Penguin Group Ireland, 25 St. Stephen's Green, Dublin 2, Ireland (a division of Penguin Books Ltd.)
Penguin Group (Australia), 250 Camberwell Road, Camberwell, Victoria 3124, Australia
(a division of Pearson Australia Group Pty. Ltd.)
Penguin Books India Pvt. Ltd., 11 Community Centre, Panchsheel Park, New Delhi—110 017, India
Penguin Group (NZ), 67 Apollo Drive, Rosedale, North Shore 0632, New Zealand
(a division of Pearson New Zealand Ltd.)
Penguin Books (South Africa) (Pty.) Ltd., 24 Sturdee Avenue, Rosebank, Johannesburg 2196,
South Africa

Penguin Books Ltd., Registered Offices: 80 Strand, London WC2R 0RL, England

While the author has made every effort to provide accurate telephone numbers and Internet addresses at the time of publication, neither the publisher nor the author assumes any responsibility for errors, or for changes that occur after publication. Further, the publisher does not have any control over and does not assume any responsibility for author or third-party websites or their content.

Copyright © 2010 by Paul Owens and Brad Crawford
Text design by Tiffany Estreicher

First edition: February 2010

Library of Congress Cataloging-in-Publication Data

Owens, Paul, 1970–
    The little green book of absinthe : an essential companion with lore, trivia, and classic and contemporary cocktails / Paul Owens and Paul Nathan ; drink recipes by Dave Herlong.
        p.   cm.
    Includes index.
    ISBN 978-0-399-53563-5
    1. Cocktails.   2. Absinthe.   3. Drinking customs—History.   I. Nathan, Paul, 1963–   II. Herlong, Dave.   III. Title.
    TX951.O975 2010
    641.8′74—dc22   2009038235

PRINTED IN THE UNITED STATES OF AMERICA

10   9   8   7   6   5   4   3   2   1

The recipes contained in this book are to be followed exactly as written. The publisher is not responsible for your specific health or allergy needs that may require medical supervision. The publisher is not responsible for any adverse reactions to the recipes contained in this book.

Most Perigee books are available at special quantity discounts for bulk purchases for sales promotions, premiums, fund-raising, or educational use. Special books, or book excerpts, can also be created to fit specific needs. For details, write: Special Markets, Penguin Group (USA) Inc., 375 Hudson Street, New York, New York 10014.

To the passionate and intrepid members of
the absinthe community who have so selflessly
shared their observations, preferences, and expertise.
May your sense of taste never fail.

CONTENTS

INTRODUCTION

Absinthe means trouble. The forbidden drink. The green fairy. The absinthe murders. Muse of poets, painters, and revolutionaries. So dangerous that the United States banned it in 1912, four years before cocaine and heroin.

So naturally, now that absinthe again flows unchecked in bars across the United States and Europe, Las Vegas—the original town of swagger, rebellion, and naughty weekend adventures—has adopted the spirit as its own. Vegas means trouble, and legal absinthe hit the place like three cherries on a $100 slot.

But in Vegas, where nothing stays unadulterated for long, absinthe wasn't likely to remain traditional, paired with sugar and ice water and served in an absinthe glass. In a flash of inspiration, Dave Herlong, master mixologist at the Palms Resort & Casino, began mixing it into cocktails. It was a new twist on an old idea. Absinthe began appearing in American cocktails a good forty years before the 1912 ban, most often dashed in to spice up mixed drinks. The Sazerac, America's most famous early cocktail, was a New Orleans creation made with rye whiskey, bitters, and an absinthe rinse. By 1900, adding absinthe to mixed drinks became so common that George Kappeler, a prominent barkeep of the era, wrote, "The free use of absinthe is injurious. Never serve it in any kind of drink unless called for by the customer."

It may have been uncalled for, but injurious? Plenty of experts at the time—doctors, politicians, preachers—bleated about the risks of something called "absinthism," akin to alcoholism but apparently more depraved. Chemists said the culprit was thujone, a neurotoxin found in grande wormwood (*Artemisia absinthium*, the ingredient that gives absinthe its name) that caused seizures, hallucinations, and brain damage. They were right about thujone: in high doses, it's lethal. But they were wrong about absinthe. It contains very little thujone. Any danger in absinthe comes from alcohol, not poisonous plants.

Prior to 1920 the only mixers were water, tonic, and perhaps a bit of lemon during the summer. Even ice was available only in limited quantities. Drink mixers came into vogue early in the twentieth century, and bartenders began focusing as much on the mixers as on the alcohol. Gin, for instance, has lost all hints of the juniper plant for which it was named, but as it has morphed into a neutral spirit, it has become easier to mix into a wider range of cocktails.

In Vegas, Dave Herlong's innovation has been to combine

the fleet of mixers we have today with moderately spiced absinthe. His first creation was a variation on the vodka-based Lemon Drop, which large parties at the Palms began ordering two and three rounds of as a shot—an unheard-of order even around the high-stakes tables. Dave christened it the Gargoyle, the watcher and protector. He calls it his "mother sauce," the starting point for dozens of other recipes, all included here. You can add most anything to it: fresh muddled fruits, juices, liqueurs, and other liquors. There are many others unrelated to the Gargoyle, of course: frozen drinks and hot drinks, punches and spritzers, martinis and rickeys, 117 in all. Each of the five sections contains some absolute favorites, the ones you have to try, serve, and then recommend to others—indicated with an embellishment on the recipe's title.

The idea of capturing this new breed of absinthe cocktail in a book took root at parties and bars in San Francisco, including Paul Owens's restaurant, Tortilla Heights, as he and Paul Nathan watched what absinthe drinkers liked and what bartenders were experimenting with. The two of them—actually the two of us—met at one of Nathan's absinthe parties not long before the California Department of Alcoholic Beverage Control and local police busted him for selling absinthe. To this day, Nathan and his bartenders remain the only people arrested for selling absinthe during America's ninety-five-year ban.

We both discovered real absinthe in the 1990s in our separate travels through Europe, and our passion for absinthe comes in large part from those experiences. But fair warning: this is not a book for purists (thankfully, since neither of us can claim to be pure). We candidly and gratefully acknowledge the true history of absinthe, which in more recent times has been co-opted for dubious purposes, but at the same time we refuse to restrict ourselves to what's been done in the past. Our long-ago predecessors felt the same way, which is why we have innovations like absinthe spoons and fountains and the incredible variety of recipes from country to country that you see today. Let's broaden our horizons. The days gone by . . . have gone by. The world's most illicit spirit has been turned loose, and it shows no signs of staying in Vegas.

ABSINTHE
ESSENTIALS

Absinthe ads like to trade on artists like Van Gogh and Toulouse-Lautrec, as if the history of the green fairy began in the Pigalle neighborhood of 1870s Paris, but wormwood-infused drinks have been around for thousands of years. Egyptian physicians were using them as antiseptics and cures for

THE ORIGINAL GREEN GODDESS

The scientific name for wormwood, *Artemisia absinthium*, might have come from the Greek goddess of the forest, fertility, and the hunt, Artemis, who was said to have delivered it to the centaur Chiron, a great healer, to use as medicine. Aside from using wormwood to treat cramps and certain types of disease, many cultures historically believed it could protect the genitals and promote fertility.

intestinal worms and stomachaches before King Tut. In ancient Greece, Olympic champions drank wine mixed with bitter wormwood as a reminder to remain humble in victory. And during the Middle Ages, Europeans infused beers and wines with wormwood to make health tonics.

Until the early 1600s, Europe's public houses didn't deal in

HERBS AND DISTILLATION

For all the mystique surrounding absinthe as a cultural symbol, the drink itself starts innocently enough, as a neutral spirit usually made from grapes or grains. It gets mixed with a robust blend of macerated herbs, distilled and, depending on the recipe, steeped with additional herbs to add flavor and the telltale olive green color. A second, less desirable option is to mix herbal essences and artificial flavor and coloring into an alcohol base without distillation. This is the common Czech style of manufacturing. It's less expensive, but it loses some of the nuanced flavors that come from steeping intact plants. Distillers use a range of herbs that's almost culinary (see page 34 for an extensive list of traditional ingredients).

Like fine wines, there's a great diversity and subtlety to the best absinthes, and they require the same fresh ingredients, precise proportions, careful tending during distillation, and appropriate storage once in the bottle. Every brand is different, but a proper absinthe should have green anise, which contributes a licorice flavor and the *louche*; fennel, which has a more subdued and complementary licorice flavor; and grande wormwood, which contributes the bitterness and controversy. Some absinthes use petite wormwood (also called southern wormwood or southwood), which is a fine addition but not a substitute for grande wormwood.

spirits, only beer and wine. Liquor was primarily the domain of chemists and apothecaries. Absinthe shares those medicinal roots, despite being a relative latecomer to the bartender's shelf. As the legend goes, a French doctor, Pierre Ordinaire, invented it as a cure-all in Couvet, Switzerland, where he had fled the French Revolution in the 1780s. He was a tall, eccentric man who made his appointed rounds on an undersized horse named Roquette and experimented with a tonic of wormwood, anise, hyssop, melissa, chamomile, and other herbs steeped in alcohol. The resulting tincture became popular in the region, farm country where locals hailed it as a cure-all. Dr. Ordinaire's housekeeper and lover was said to have sold his recipe for wider production after his death.

If you think this version of events sounds too perfect, you're probably right. The Swiss had been distilling something close to absinthe since at least the 1750s, and Mère Henriod (the housekeeper of legend) and her sister had been making it before Dr. Ordinaire arrived in Couvet. It seems only too convenient that a French doctor rode in, if not on his high horse, then one with a grandiose name, and in the course of a few years created a medicine from local plants that Couvet's residents had until then merely been admiring from afar. The people of Couvet were farmers who were more likely to know the mountainside flora and its uses than a late-coming expatriate. Dr. Ordinaire may well have played a role in popularizing absinthe, but his tale of invention smells like French revisionist history. Unfortunately, we have little better to go on. In absinthe, we see what we want to see.

What we do know for sure is that one of the Henriod sisters' customers, Major Henri Dubied, was especially enthusiastic about the drink and bought the recipe in 1797. (In some versions of the story, Dr. Ordinaire lived on and sold the recipe himself.) After some experimentation, he opened a small commercial distillery the next year in Couvet with his son-in-law, Henri-Louis Pernod. Like Dr. Ordinaire, Major Dubied was French and began tapping his contacts in the French military to spur sales. Disease was always a hazard in those days, and soldiers, their immune systems compromised by physical rigor, cramped living quarters, and exotic germs, were among the most vulnerable.

Absinthe sales took off from the start, and in 1805 Pernod invested his share of the profits in a new distillery just over the French border in Pontarlier, only sixteen miles from Couvet. France had the bigger sales potential, and by setting up his distillery in Pontarlier, Pernod could avoid the import taxes levied on Swiss-made absinthe.

Distillation turned out to be crucial to absinthe's commercial success. An absinthe made with water or mixed with beer would have had a limited shelf life. In a tincture, alcohol preserved the concentrated botanical oils—the same oils that fall out of suspension to create the cloudy *louche* that appears when you add water. Stored in cool, dark, sealed bottles, absinthe can maintain potency for decades. Entrepreneurs, in fact, are still finding and selling rare caches of vintage absinthe that can fetch thousands of dollars per bottle.

When the French invaded Algeria in 1830, Pernod Fils (Pernod and Sons) absinthe went with them. To combat malaria, soldiers stationed in Algiers received daily rations of absinthe for their drinking water, a field cocktail they enhanced with sugar when they could get it. It was an acquired taste, but once acquired, it stuck, and French forces occupied Algeria for decades. Upon returning home, soldiers began asking for absinthe in cafés, and since the French had rarely won wars, civilians took a certain heady pride in ordering the same drink as their successful military men. "I'll have what he's having" was the sentiment of the times.

ABSINTHE ORDINAIRE

This recipe for Absinthe Ordinaire represents a typical distillation formula from the late nineteenth century. "Ordinaire" in this case refers to the approximate level of alcohol in the finished product, not to Pierre Ordinaire, the fabled creator of absinthe.

Grande wormwood, dried and cleaned	2.5 kilograms
Hyssop flower, dried	500 grams
Citronated melissa, dried	500 grams
Green anise, crushed	2 kilograms
Alcohol (85 degrees)	16 liters

Infuse the entire cucurbit for twenty-four hours, add 15 liters of water, and distill carefully to produce 15 liters of product, adding:

Alcohol (85 degrees)	40 liters
Ordinary water	45 liters

Produces 100 liters at 45 degrees; mix and let rest.

—Translated from *Traité de la Fabrication des Liqueurs*, 1882

Already absinthe was displaying a remarkable ability to be everything to everyone. Created in the country, it had taken hold with the military and then urbanites, the respectable middle class who saw it as a tasty, healthful, patriotic drink. As its popularity grew, distillers less reputable than Pernod found ways to produce knockoff absinthes that skirted the intensive, expensive production processes authentic absinthe required. The low-grade absinthes used cheap flavorings and cheaper alcohol. The poorer classes flocking to Paris for factory work adopted these low-grade absinthes, which sometimes contained questionable and even poisonous additives.

Authentic absinthe's crisp herbal flavor gave it an immediate advantage over other spirits of the day. Cocktails as we know them didn't really come into their own until after World War I. Early versions would look Spartan to our eyes: minimal garnish, bitters, perhaps water and a little sugar to cut the spirits. Imagine drinking straight gin at room temperature in the middle of summer. Not very refreshing. But absinthe mixed with water, even without ice or sugar, even lukewarm, hit the spot. Absinthe had crossed the line from tonic to tipple.

Absinthe notched another gain in the 1860s, when an insect plague decimated France's grape crops and put the price of wine beyond reach of all but the well heeled. Drinking wine became a conspicuous statement of means, even as winemakers raged against absinthe's rise.

The era was as dynamic as the absinthe. Few periods in history have matched the late 1800s and early 1900s—the Belle

Époque period in France—for advancements in science and engineering. The wealth of technologies nurtured an unprecedented culture of art, fashion, theater, and high living that we're still aspiring to today. Photography, haute couture, international exhibitions, and Impressionism all came out of the age. The talented and the talentless crowded into Paris's cafés and salons to discuss art theories, flaunt their intellects, and, of course, drink. Absinthe was hardly the exclusive domain of artists, but the combination of unusual color, the hypnotic spirals of milky yellow *louche* following a water drip, and its clear-headed buzz endeared it to Parisian creatives as an object of almost mystical worship.

Notably, the absinthe of a hundred years earlier had displayed the same properties but hadn't been shrouded in mystery in the same way. Part of the Belle Époque attraction was the ritual itself (see "Good *Louche*: The Absinthe Ritual"). The more popular absinthe got, the more formalized the ritual became. (Swiss farmers surely weren't using absinthe spoons and carafes of ice water back in Couvet, nor were the French soldiers, the *Zouaves*, in Algeria.) A careful preparation required adding the water drop by drop and attentively appreciating the pattern of the *louche* and the release of the oils' aromatics. Writers often speak of "entering the page," a short, personal ritual performed to find the right frame of mind for writing, and the meditative mixing of absinthe could have served the same purpose for the artists of the day.

There was also a darker side to the preoccupation with

GOOD *LOUCHE*: THE ABSINTHE RITUAL

Traditionally, absinthe was served by pouring an ounce in a glass, then topping off with three to five parts cold water. Some of the low-stemmed absinthe glasses have a bulb shape at the bottom specifically to cue the pourer on the proper dose: when the bulb is full, you're ready to add water.

If you take it with sugar, which you'll probably want to if you're drinking a *verte* (French-style) absinthe, you'll need a slotted, trowel-shaped absinthe spoon to place across the rim of the glass to make it the traditional way. Set a sugar cube on the spoon, and slowly drip ice-cold water over the sugar and into the glass. Absinthe fountains provide a slow, steady drip of water. A *brouilleur*, a glass or metal cup that fits atop the glass to drip the water automatically, offers an elegant option to the traditional ritual.

Pouring slowly, if you're using cubed sugar, gives the water a chance to dissolve it, and gives you a chance to observe the *louche*. An experienced *absintheur* can identify a brand from across the room just by watching how it *louches*—how the herbs' oils cloud the drink as you add water. Absinthe's exceptionally high alcohol content (50 to 80 percent) isn't gratuitous. It keeps those oils in suspension. The higher the alcohol content, the more oils the absinthe can hold, and the more flavor you release by diluting it. Some of the most complex absinthes tend to have more alcohol, though a high alcohol content alone is not a reliable indicator of fine absinthe.

The other secret of the *louche* is that different plant oils fall out of suspension at different concentrations so that, as you add water, every absinthe reveals secrets about the herbs it holds and offers hints on how to pour. Anise is responsible for the *louche*. An absinthe heavy on anise and light on other botanicals will appear to *louche* suddenly and more uniformly. A more broadly herbed absinthe will *louche* in twisting, cascading trails that trace the path of your dripping water. (See clips of different styles of absinthe *louch-*

ing at www.absintheparty.com.) In most mixed drinks you won't notice a *louche* amidst all the opaque mixers, but normally transparent cocktails paired with heavy-*louching* absinthes might appear milky.

If you're the daring type, you may want to pour your absinthe Bohemian style. Bohemian-style, or Czech-style, absinthes draw a lot of criticism for not being authentic and not containing enough anise, but that's not fair. They should instead be criticized because they generally taste horrible. (See "Good Taste: Mixing Absinthe Cocktails" on page 13 for more on Bohemian absinthe.) Nevertheless, the Bohemian ritual, while not historically authentic, has established a place in absinthe lore, and if you wish to punish yourself, we won't judge you.

To drink Bohemian style, pour a bit of chilled water into the glass, place an absinthe spoon across the rim of the glass, and put a sugar cube on the spoon. Pour a measure of absinthe over the sugar cube and light the cube on fire. Admire the dancing flame. Let the sugar burn until it begins to turn brown, and then slowly pour the rest of your water over the cube. Take special care when lighting because alcohol has a blue flame that's not always easy to see but will burn you and your loose shirtsleeves just the same. So will smoldering sugar and hot glass. Whether you pour Bohemian absinthe or another style, use something that's at least 120 proof, or you'll have trouble lighting it.

absinthe. With such widespread admiration of arts and culture, artists competed intensely, outwardly or more subtly, to produce the most original, provocative, and fashionable ideas and looked for every edge they could get. Absinthe was like artistic steroids. Nearly everyone in France was drinking it at the time, but for creatives it was more than an aperitif. It was a symbol and a tool, the key to an elevated consciousness and an effortless bloom of ideas—the green muse.

The artists well knew it was an empty gambit, even as they hoped against hope. A common joke was of the hapless artist who needed seven absinthes to find his genius, but only ever had money enough to buy six. Or the muse might cut the other way, as Edmond Bourgeois wrote in a poem about drinking for inspiration: "It needed only one glass, and I drank two."

Whether absinthe helped or hurt, it's undeniably true that some of the greatest artists of the age drank it, and drank it heavily, as they produced their iconic works. Edouard Manet's *Absinthe Drinker* ushered in the Impressionist era. Van Gogh's *Still Life with Absinthe* displays the characteristic yellow tones that showed up in so many of his paintings, said to be influenced by the color of absinthe. Some of France's greatest poets were notorious absinthe drinkers: Alfred de Musset, Charles Baudelaire, Paul Verlaine, Arthur Rimbaud. For them, absinthe might not have been indisputably good, but life without it would have been unthinkable.

Soon after, absinthe would enter a gray zone. Still popular, in the 1890s it began to face increasing disapproval from the upper classes, led by the wine industry and the temperance movement. Edgar Degas's masterpiece *L'Absinthe* was booed off the auction block unsold at Christie's in London. Absinthe was blamed for the essential breakdown of society. Belgium banned it in 1906, Switzerland in 1910, the United States in 1912, France in 1915.

If absinthe isn't banned, our country will rapidly become an immense padded cell where half the Frenchmen will be occupied putting straight jackets on the other half.

—GEORGES OHNET, 1907

At the time, science suggested that absinthe represented a real danger to imbibers, one that naïve or negligent citizens needed protection from. The explanations had the sheen of truth, but the underlying reasons were mythical. The governments, winemakers, and religious teetotalers invented a history and persona for absinthe no less vivid and effective than the myths of the artists and writers.

Still, the mystique would mean little if absinthe didn't also captivate in the glass. And for it to do that, you'll need to know your way around the bar.

Good Taste:
Mixing Absinthe Cocktails

If you're the kind of person who enjoys gourmet wines, chocolates, or coffees, you'll probably get excited by absinthe's wide range of flavors. The spectrum is broad, and flavors overlap and diverge to an astounding degree. Even the same brand can differ vastly from year to year and bottle to bottle, especially artisanal brands.

There are three basic styles: Swiss, French, and Bohemian or Czech. The Swiss, French, and Bohemian monikers are not bound by geography. An American absinthe can be Swiss, a Spanish absinthe can be French, and a German absinthe can be Bohemian, if you follow us. To clear that up, in the chart below we refer to Swiss absinthes as *blanches* and French absinthes as *vertes*. The Bohemians are on their own. Note that as of this writing, there are no Bohemian-style absinthes being sold legally in the United States, but we've included two in the chart for comparison, and in the recipes, since they can be bought online.

A fourth category of absinthe has emerged in recent years, a category of one. Le Tourment Vert is billed as authentically French but in fact is an American absinthe in taste and market appeal. Those who enjoy drinking a glass of absinthe the traditional way would probably find little reason to pick up a bottle, but it distinguishes itself as a mixer. At 100 proof and with some sugars in the bottle, it straddles the line between liquor and liqueur; there's little anise, which makes it more agreeable to the American palate, and more mint and citrus. We think of it as the first cocktail absinthe, and as such we return to it frequently in recipes because of its supple character and ability to play nicely with many different flavors. Other, stronger absinthes get the call when we want absinthe's flavor center stage.

With so many different styles, and even tastes within each style, you might ask yourself, *Will a cocktail made with Lucid taste like the same cocktail made with Obsello?* No. Not even close. Because of that, each recipe calls for a specific brand and type. You can use absinthes other than what's listed, but know that you're striking out into the realm of experimentation. We encourage that and include this tasting chart to guide you in your choices. You will notice that we rarely call for a premium absinthe, a sipping absinthe, in a recipe for the same reason that you wouldn't mix your twelve-year Scotch with Coke.

The Swiss brands tend to be lighter and mix well with more subtle flavors and other liquors. They make great martinis and spritzers, are easily drinkable without sugar, and add nuance to a drink that you might otherwise mix using gin or vodka. French brands are almost always more bitter but also tend to be more complex and interesting. They mix well with fruit drinks, especially sweet fruits, as the bitterness and sugar complement one another. French brands are also great with punch for the same reason. We tend to use French styles in place of whiskeys for mixing. They also work well in place of rum, but you may need to add some sugar or simple syrup to the mix. Bohemian absinthes tend to be even more bitter and less complex than French, and contain little or no anise. Some say they aren't absinthes at all, having come out of the Czech Republic in the early nineties with no ties to the pre-ban communities of distillers. When there's a call to substitute an outside brand for the one listed in the recipe, favor absinthes in the same category: Swiss absinthes can substitute for other Swiss, French for French, and Bohemian for Bohemian, with some tweaking of proportions to taste. When swapping out Tourment, it's best to lean toward a Swiss style.

Now excuse us while we step over to mix up some cocktails . . .

BRANDS	ORIGIN	STYLE	BACKGROUND
Clandestine	Switzerland	*Blanche*	A former bootleg absinthe from the legendary Val-de-Travers region, birthplace of absinthe, distilled by Artemisia-Bugnon. One of the first to be licensed for sale after the Swiss ban was lifted.
La Fée Absinth Bohemian	UK, but distilled and bottled in the Czech Republic	Bohemian	If a Bohemian-style comes to the United States, this will probably be the first, and one of the best of that style.
La Fée Absinthe Parisienne	UK, but distilled and bottled in Paris	*Verte*	First French-style absinthe to be manufactured since the French ban in 1915 and first absinthe to be really marketed outside of the Czech Republic.
Hill's	Czech Republic	Bohemian	Bitter and aquamarine, Hill's is only nominally absinthe but did hit on a latent fascination with absinthe's traditions and lore that paved the way for a revival. Not yet sold in the United States.
Kübler	Switzerland	*Blanche*	Yves Kübler, grandson of the distillery's founder, led the return of legal absinthe to Switzerland in 2005, and later to the United States. All its herbs are grown in the Val-de-Travers region.
Lucid	France	*Verte*	First modern absinthe to be sold in America since the ban in 1912. Forensically re-created by Ted Breaux, maker of the vaunted Jade line of absinthes.
Obsello	Spain	*Verte*	A French-style absinthe created by two American expats living near Barcelona.
Pernod	France	*Verte*	The most popular historical absinthe recovers from its pastis phase to produce an enjoyable post-ban drink.
St. George	United States	*Verte*	First absinthe manufactured in America since the ban in 1912.
Le Tourment Vert	United States, but distilled and bottled in Cognac, France	American	Made with the US market in mind. Billed as "authentically French" but in fact is the first cocktail absinthe.

TASTE	BEST WHEN ...
Crisp and mellow. Anise and fennel are there, but in a delicate balance with a chorus of other herbs.	Whenever. Clandestine is almost uniquely versatile, as good in a glass as in any mixed drink. Substitutes easily for any Kübler or Tourment recipe.
No anise, no *louche*, very bitter, and high in alcohol.	Mixed in sweet or fruity drinks that might be thrown off by too much anise or floral flavor. Dilute liberally.
Heavy on the anise and alcoholic. *Louches* well but with little in the way of other herbals.	Dripped with sugar or served in a fizz or in fruity cocktails.
Overpowering mint and very high alcohol content.	Poured out. Alternatively, pour an ounce with a sugar cube into a small-mouth rocks glass. Light it and quickly put your hand over the top to seal in the fumes. With the flame out, break the seal, huff the fumes, and shoot the rest. Repeat as needed to induce unconsciousness.
Bright, crisp anise and fennel flavors. Short finish with hints of wormwood and mint. Straightforward and mild. *Louche* is strong and immediate.	Served in the ritual or mixed with Champagne, coffee, or minty cocktails.
Prominent anise, subtle wormwood, and strong pepper and coriander. Naturally colored with solid, distinctive *louche*.	Mixed in spiced drinks like Bloody Marys or winter toddies, and in vermouth-based cocktails.
Light and simple, with anise and herbs.	Mixed with Champagne, in light spritzers, and in citrus cocktails. We like it in the Death in the Afternoon.
Commanding anise at the fore, followed by notes of citrus and lemon balm that dissipate quickly. Robust *louche*.	Mixed in citrus-heavy cocktails and/or balanced by a liqueur or rich liquor, such as spiced rum.
Layered and complex. A bit bitter at the finish.	Mixed in high-ingredient cocktails with amaretto or grenadine, or traditional cocktails with bitters.
Almost no anise. Contains citrus, mint, and eucalyptus.	Mixed. Tourment is the most versatile of these absinthes, and with its lower alcohol content and milder flavor can be mixed more heavily if you wish.

Cocktail Nuts and Bolts

There are five primary ways to make a cocktail, but nearly all of the drinks included here call for one of two ways: building or shaking. Building a drink simply means that you make it in the glass it will be drunk from, usually with ice. Liquid ingredients are measured and poured in the order shown on the recipe list; citrus wedges, if the drink calls for any, get squeezed and dropped in, and the drink is stirred briefly with a sip stick to blend everything together. At the end comes the garnish.

Shaking is a bit more involved. Many of the martinis and some of the other drinks contain fruit juices, and these need to be shaken to get the juices properly integrated with the absinthe and other ingredients. The same goes for drinks with milk or egg, like the Absinthe Suissesse or Absinthe Fizz. The Boston shaker, a two-part affair with a metal half and a glass half, is the professional standard because it's easier to handle and gives you more room to work with. You can also use a standard metal shaker with a lid and strainer at the top. You'll fill the standard shaker, or the glass portion of a Boston shaker, two-thirds full of ice (muddling any ingredients in the bottom first), add the liquid ingredients, and shake with authority for about twenty seconds. The longer you shake, the more diluted the drink becomes. If you prefer a stronger drink (not usually advisable, since the absinthe relies on water to release its full flavor), try using larger ice cubes rather than cutting back on the shake. A proper shake requires a good ten seconds at least.

MEASURING

1 dash	= $\frac{1}{32}$ ounce
1 teaspoon	= $\frac{1}{8}$ ounce
1 splash*	= $\frac{1}{8}$ ounce
1 tablespoon	= $\frac{3}{8}$ ounce
Float (unless otherwise listed)	= $\frac{1}{2}$ ounce
1 pony	= 1 ounce
1 jigger	= 1½ ounces (standard bar shot)
1 split	= 6 ounces
1 cup	= 8 ounces
1 pint	= 2 cups (16 ounces)
1 quart	= 4 cups (32 ounces)

* That most maddening of measurements, the splash can be anything from $\frac{1}{32}$ ounce to ¼ ounce depending on who's talking. We peg it at $\frac{1}{8}$ ounce but say *splash* to allow you to pour to taste. And when you're working at home without a speed pourer, a splash is necessarily an inexact measurement. Behind the bar it works out to about half a count.

You're done when the outside is covered in condensation. Drinks with egg or cream-based liqueurs need twice as many shakes as normal. You'll then strain the drink into a glass to filter out extra ice that would overly dilute your mixture. In a Boston shaker you can do this with a separate strainer, or you can just slip apart the glass and metal portions enough to let the liquid trickle through into a drinking glass.

Layering is a less common—and some would argue more frustrating—way to make a cocktail. Here the drink is not mixed but laid down ingredient by ingredient into a glass to be drunk the same way you'd eat dinner courses. Every layer but the first has to be added with care to avoid disturbing the layer below it, and the order of your pours matters more than ever—the heaviest liquids must go on the bottom. To layer, you can hold a bar spoon upside down over the glass and allow the liquid to gently trickle in, or, if layering is especially difficult, you can drip the float down the side of a slightly tilted glass or down a cocktail stick touching the side of the glass. Much more frequently than layering, our drinks call for a float—the last liquid ingredient added to a drink and one that floats on top as a separate layer. This is more about flavor than appearance and need not be quite as exact as, say, the intricate layers of a Pousse Café you might see on the cover of a gourmet magazine.

For frozen drinks, you'll want to add the absinthe and other liquid ingredients and purée any fruit before adding ice. The ice itself should be crushed or shaved; most blenders aren't capable of quickly breaking down cubed or cracked ice to the smooth consistency you'll need. (You might need to enlist the services of an ice crusher or hammer and towel.) Once the ice is in, start the blender on a low setting and work your way up the ladder until the ice is completely blended and smooth.

A few drinks here, like the Champagne cocktails, will do with a simple stir. A bar spoon works well. Stirring both mixes the ingredients and, when they contain ice, chills the drink. For Champagne cocktails and other drinks with carbonation, stir gently and only enough to mix it, in order to keep the drink from getting flat.

Other tips and tricks:

- Ice is a drink's most important ingredient. It should be fresh, made with filtered or bottled water, and still frosty while you're making the drink. Unless otherwise specified, cracked or cubed ice will suffice for these recipes, cracked ice chilling the drink faster and adding more water, cubed ice less so. Frozen drinks, frappés, and the Suissesse take crushed or shaved ice. (Bartenders will sometimes speak of "frappée-ing a glass," which in laymen's terms just means to put shaved ice in it.)

- Ice aside, great ingredients make a great cocktail. Use fresh, and freshly cut, fruits and garnishes whenever possible.

- Unless it's a hot drink, serve it in a chilled glass. This will keep the drink cold longer, offset the heat coming from your hand, and generally yield a more pleasant drinking experience.

- If you're making drinks for more than one person, multiply the recipe's measurements and make them all at the same time so that everyone's tastes the same. Pour around to each glass twice to keep portions even and equalize any disparities in the mixture from top to bottom.

- A pro bartender might snort, but we like Oxo's mini angled measuring cups for measuring at home. Jiggers often don't list their sizes, and half a jigger is harder to eyeball with its conical shape. Oxo's cups are clear so you can measure from the side as well as the top, and they come labeled with British and metric markings.

- For drinks containing egg, the egg should always go into your shaker before the liquor. Make sure it's fresh, and use only the egg white. If you have butterfingers, separate the yolk over another container, and then pour the white into your glass. Cocktails with egg or any milky ingredients should get some extra shakes once everything's poured.

- Yuzu, a Japanese citrus fruit whose juice appears in a few recipes, can be hard to find. The fruit is available in the United States seasonally (September through January). Juices and frozen fruit can be found year-round at Japanese markets.

Garnishes

Garnishes do three things: they add flavor and visual appeal, and they define the character of the drink. Consider the difference between a spritzer that has a cherry and a lemon twist as garnish and one with a lemon wedge, pineapple spear, umbrella, and three plastic monkeys hanging off the rim. Absinthe and citrus go together like peas and carrots, so most garnishes in this book use lemon, lime, or orange garnishes, but by no means all at once. The garnish repertoire is large and includes vegetables (olives, celery, chili peppers), spices (nutmeg, cinnamon sticks, pepper), and confections (powdered sugar, chocolate). *The Little Green Book* itself garnishes the Red Leather with Fruit Roll-Ups, and our Lava Lamp uses gelatin.

Whether you use the listed garnish or come up with your own, make sure it complements the drink, and garnish sparingly. A few notes on our garnishes:

WEDGE: Unlike the slice and wheel, the citrus wedge is cut from stem to tip (or navel), usually in eighths. Sometimes a drink will call for two—one squeezed and tossed in the bottom of the drink, and one cut with a horizontal notch to nest on the rim of the glass.

WHEEL: Wheels are full cross sections of limes, lemons, or oranges, about one-eighth- to one-quarter-inch thick. Trim the first half inch or so off each end before you get to the meat of the fruit, cut the wheels, and slice to the center of the fruit, leaving the other half intact to hold the wheel on the rim of a glass. Wheels can be dropped into a drink but are more aesthetic than practical. If you hope to use some of the juice in your drink, the wedge is your garnish.

SLICE: Slices are half wheels that can be crosscut to nest on the rim or uncut if tossed directly into a drink, as they often are with punches and toddies.

TWIST: Twists are often thought of as decorative garnishes, but the act of twisting wrings oils from the peel and adds a subtle flavor. Rub the twist around the rim of the glass before you drop it in. The key to cutting attractive citrus twists is a channel knife, also known as a zester. A channel knife makes uniform one-eighth-inch strips—no ice picks, paring knives, or cut fingertips necessary. Alternatively, you can use a vegetable peeler for a less artful but equally functional garnish. Either way, take care to cut only the peel and not the white pith underneath.

Flag: The flag, or sail, is a thin citrus wheel folded in half around a small garnish, usually a cherry, and is speared with a cocktail stick. Depending on which way you hold it, the cocktail stick and citrus look like a ship's mast and sail. A variation is the twist flag, which simply combines the twist and the flag. The twist can run in a crescent shape around the center fruit or spiral around the cocktail stick.

Small garnishes: Small garnishes meant to sit on top of the drink, like raspberries, grapes, or olives, can take a spear or cocktail stick to hold them above the fray. If a recipe calls for two in-drink garnishes, like a cherry and a lemon, enlist a cocktail stick to hold them together.

Rim garnishes: Salted and sugared rims are garnishes too. Use a citrus wedge or whatever garnish the drink calls for to moisten the rim, turn the glass upside down in a ring of salt or sugar, and twist it until the rim is well covered.

TALL
COCKTAILS

*It is the most delicate and trembling of
all vestments, this drunkenness by virtue of the
sagebrush of the glaciers, absomphe.*

—ARTHUR RIMBAUD

Perhaps because tall cocktails have a bit more real estate to fill (each drink is about six ounces pre-garnish) and most contain ice, they tend to make good spring and summer drinks: lighter, refreshing, flexible blends designed for casual socializing and cooling off near pools, barbecue grills, beaches, and golf courses. True to their easygoing nature, these are also drinks that can accept many different kinds of absinthes. Pour your preference, and stock up on lemons and limes. Highlights: Absinthe Fizz, Bloody Margaux.

POSTCARD FROM COUVET

If you ever have the chance to visit Couvet, in the Val-de-Travers region less than fifteen miles away from the French–Swiss border, you owe it to yourself to go. It looks exactly how you'd expect a Swiss hamlet to look: tidy, intimate, beige buildings completely in keeping with the surrounding mountainous landscape. There's only one road through town, but they've had to build five or six houses in the past few years to keep up with the uptick in population—now about 2,750. The nearest big city is Bern, an hour east.

The big draw of the Val-de-Travers is its status as the birthplace of absinthe. Père François has a museum in the village of Motiers that houses one of the largest private collections of absinthe paraphernalia in the world: pre-ban bottles, fountains, spoons, glassware, stills, and ephemera. He also makes a strikingly good Swiss absinthe.

The French-speaking Val-de-Travers is filled with old stills once used to make bootleg absinthe during Switzerland's ban. Some may still be used for the sake of avoiding registration and taxes. Residents are friendly but careful about discussing such things. Among Americans, the most famous brands made here are Kübler and Clandestine. Until a few years ago Clandestine was an underground operation whose name itself is another word for *bootleg*. Looking around, you realize just how important making absinthe is to the people and the region. If the rest of the world forgot about absinthe tomorrow, the Val-de-Travers would go on as it always has. There would simply be little or no commercial absinthe.

The scale of production is probably the biggest change in recent years. Since absinthe was legalized, first in the EU and later in the States, wormwood production around Couvet and across the border in Pontarlier, France, has grown from a few plants in backyard herb gardens to acre upon acre of commercial fields. Five primary farms in the region grow grande wormwood, mint, peppermint, petit wormwood, melissa, and other herbs. Wormwood especially loves the sunny, relatively dry mountain climate (Couvet's elevation is almost 2,500 feet). Wormwood plants here yield twelve times as much essential oil as those grown in other regions. Anise and fennel, the two other key herbs, can't survive the high altitude and short growing season, though; anise comes from Spain, and most of the fennel from the south of France.

The farmers plant, weed, and harvest wormwood by hand. Farmers work approximately 1,200 hours for each acre of wormwood planted. Come the August harvest, the plants can reach more than a meter high. They head to a drying room, where warm forced air quickly dries them to prevent mold and mildew. Once dry, they are chopped, bagged, and shipped to distillers around the world. (Master distillers use botanicals from several different years to maintain a consistent flavor from batch to batch.)

The system, season by season, rolls on much as it always has. Just watching a harvest brings everything into sharper focus, and at the same time reveals a glimpse of the bigger picture. You can't come up to Couvet and participate in the tastings and traditions without realizing that, small point on the map or no, it sits squarely at the center of the world of absinthe.

Laneside Lemonade

Versatile, easy to drink, and compatible with most absinthes.

1 OUNCE GRANDE ABSENTE absinthe

2 OUNCES LEMONADE

2 OUNCES 7UP

Build in a tall glass over ice. Garnish with a lemon wedge.

Absinthe Fizz

An absinthe cocktail of the old school. No sweet-and-sour here—just, egg, fresh lemon juice, and sugar.

1½ OUNCES LUCID ABSINTHE

JUICE OF HALF A LEMON

1 TEASPOON SUGAR

1 EGG WHITE

CLUB SODA

Shake absinthe, lemon juice, sugar, and egg white very well and pour into a highball glass. Fill with club soda. Garnish with a lemon wedge. Aside from Lucid, we also recommend Le Tourment Vert, La Fée Absinthe Parisienne, and even Chartreuse. Since the base is as much about texture as taste, the fizz can go a number of different ways. To the recipe above, try adding vanilla extract, sorbet, or puréed raspberry.

Newton's Apple

This green cocktail is bursting with botanicals and juicy green apple. Neither macho nor girly, Newton has bite in the club or on the couch.

2 OUNCES GRANDE ABSENTE ABSINTHE

½ OUNCE TANQUERAY NO. TEN

1 OUNCE SOUR APPLE SCHNAPPS

2 OUNCES CLUB SODA FLOAT

Build in a tall glass filled with ice, and float club soda.

Sundance Spritzer

The spritzer, light and breezy, is an easy way to get acquainted with absinthe.

2 OUNCES LE TOURMENT VERT ABSINTHE

2 OUNCES CLUB SODA

2 OUNCES SPRITE

2 LEMON WEDGES

Build in a tall glass filled with ice. Squeeze lemon wedges and add to drink. Garnish with a third lemon wedge.

Arnold Palmer's French Caddy

The traditional Arnold Palmer (half tea and half lemonade) set the standard for summertime refreshment that the French Caddy aspires to. We think it succeeds.

2 OUNCES LE TOURMENT VERT ABSINTHE

2 OUNCES SWEET ICED TEA (OR UNSWEETENED TEA)

2 OUNCES LEMONADE

Made correctly, this is a layered cocktail with the absinthe on the bottom and the lemonade floating on top. In a tall glass filled with ice, carefully pour in the absinthe, then the tea, and finally the lemonade. Garnish with a lemon wedge.

Cucumber Breeze

Your next picnic refresher—light as a May afternoon and cool as a . . . well, you know.

2 OUNCES OBSELLO ABSINTHE

3 OUNCES CLUB SODA

1 OUNCE 7UP

2 CUCUMBER WHEELS

3 LIME WEDGES

Muddle cucumber wheels and lime wedges together and add ice and absinthe. Shake well, pour into a tall glass, and fill with club soda and 7UP. Garnish with a third cucumber wheel.

Quasimojito

Absinthe turns the rum-based mojito into a monster—but a refreshing, benevolent monster suitable for golf courses and summer patios.

2 OUNCES LE TOURMENT VERT ABSINTHE

1 OUNCE SIMPLE SYRUP

4 LEMON WEDGES

5–10 MINT LEAVES

1 SPLASH CLUB SODA

1 SPLASH 7UP

Muddle lemon wedges and mint leaves enough to bruise. Add ice, absinthe, and simple syrup, and shake well. Pour into a tall glass, and top with a splash of club soda and a splash of 7UP.

Sticker Licker

Named after Sticker, a legendary Palms bartender, the Sticker Licker is his over-the-top tropical cocktail with an absinthe kick.

1½ OUNCES LE TOURMENT VERT ABSINTHE

¾ OUNCE MALIBU RUM

1 SPLASH BLUE CURAÇAO

3 OUNCES PINEAPPLE JUICE

1 SPLASH 7UP

Shake absinthe, rum, curaçao, and pineapple juice well. Add a splash of 7UP. Pour into a large tropical glass. Garnish with a pineapple and orange wedge flag.

HERBS COMMONLY USED IN ABSINTHE

Primary	Secondary	Tertiary
green anise	melissa (lemon balm)	veronica
grande wormwood	hyssop	dittany
Florence fennel	mint	nutmeg
	peppermint	lavender
	petite wormwood (southern wormwood or southwood)	juniper
		sage
	star anise	tansy
	eucalyptus	sweet flag
	angelica	vanilla
	coriander	licorice

HEADS AND TAILS

In distillation, the first few liters of absinthe to come out of the still are called the head; the last few liters are the tail. The head and tail don't have enough alcohol to keep the oils in suspension, so the absinthe comes out of the still *louched*. The head gets thrown away, as it may contain methanol, which can cause hangovers, blindness, and death, but the tail is returned to the still for the next run.

Absinthe Margarita

The Absinthe Margarita expands on the citrusy sweet-sour Margarita to produce something richer and more floral.

2 OUNCES OBSELLO ABSINTHE

1 OUNCE TRIPLE SEC OR COINTREAU ORANGE TRIPLE SEC LIQUEUR

2 OUNCES SWEET AND SOUR MIX

1 SPLASH ORANGE JUICE

1 SPLASH FRESH LIME JUICE

Build in a tall glass, roll into a shaker, and shake well. Sugar rim and garnish with a lime wedge.

French Margarita

———

The Margarita goes north with an all-French infusion of raspberry, lime, and anise.

2 OUNCES LE TOURMENT VERT ABSINTHE

1 OUNCE COINTREAU ORANGE TRIPLE SEC LIQUEUR

1 OUNCE CHAMBORD BLACK RASPBERRY LIQUEUR

1 OUNCE SWEET AND SOUR MIX

1 SPLASH ORANGE JUICE

1 SPLASH FRESH LIME JUICE

Build in a tall glass, roll into a shaker, and shake well. Sugar rim and garnish with a raspberry and a lime wedge.

French Iguana

———

Absinthe replaces tequila in this variation of the Melon Margarita.

2 OUNCES LA FÉE ABSINTH BOHEMIAN

1 OUNCE COINTREAU ORANGE TRIPLE SEC LIQUEUR

1 OUNCE MIDORI MELON LIQUEUR

1 OUNCE SWEET AND SOUR MIX

1 SPLASH ORANGE JUICE

1 SPLASH FRESH LIME JUICE

Build in a tall glass, roll into a shaker, and shake well. Sugar rim and garnish with a lime wedge.

Bloody Margaux

Absinthe's own Bloody Mary is a natural eye-opener for Sunday-morning tailgates, or Sunday mornings period. The sauces' bold spices manage not to overwhelm Lucid's peppery tones, which remain at full volume.

2 OUNCES LUCID ABSINTHE

3 OUNCES TOMATO JUICE

2 DASHES WORCESTERSHIRE SAUCE

2 DASHES TABASCO PEPPER SAUCE

2 DASHES TABASCO GREEN PEPPER SAUCE

1 LEMON WEDGE

1 LIME WEDGE

1 DASH EACH OF BLACK PEPPER, SEA SALT, CELERY SALT

Combine all ingredients in a mixing tin filled with ice. Stir gently with a bar spoon and strain into an ice-filled tall glass. Garnish with olives and a celery stalk.

French Stormy

—

Inspired by Bermuda's traditional Dark and Stormy.

1 OUNCE ABSOLUT VODKA

½ OUNCE CAPTAIN MORGAN SPICED RUM

½ OUNCE ABSOLUT VANILIA

3 OUNCES GINGER BEER OR GINGER ALE

In a tall glass filled with ice, build the cocktail alcohol first. Top with the ginger beer (preferable to the ginger ale if you can get it). Stir with a bar spoon and garnish with an orange slice.

Green Flash

—

Hemingway's Key West–era daiquiri blended with absinthe.

2 OUNCES GRANDE ABSENTE ABSINTHE

1 OUNCE CRUZAN LIGHT RUM

1 OUNCE SIMPLE SYRUP

1 OUNCE FRESH LIME JUICE

1 OUNCE 7UP FLOAT

Shake absinthe, rum, syrup, and lime juice well and strain over ice. Float 7UP. Garnish with a lime wheel.

Green Rickey

Absinthe and elderflower deliver a bouquet to the Lime Rickey, summer's most refreshing cocktail.

1½ OUNCES TANQUERAY NO. TEN

½ OUNCE LUCID ABSINTHE

½ OUNCE FRESH LIME JUICE

½ OUNCE ROCK CANDY SYRUP

CLUB SODA

ST-GERMAIN ELDERFLOWER LIQUEUR FLOAT

Shake well, strain over ice, and top with club soda. Float St-Germain elderflower liqueur. Garnish with a lime wheel.

Blood Orange Rickey

A dark, fruity rickey that swaps the usual gin for light Swiss absinthe.

1½ OUNCES KÜBLER ABSINTHE

2 OUNCES FRESH-PRESSED BLOOD ORANGE JUICE

JUICE OF HALF A LIME

CLUB SODA

In a mixing tin, add absinthe and press the juice of one blood orange (about 2 ounces) and half a lime. Add ice and shake well. Strain into an ice-filled glass and top with club soda. Garnish with a slice of blood orange.

THE SECONDARY EFFECT

Thujone may not be much of a factor in the typical absinthe experience, but absinthe drinkers do report sensations different from other types of alcohol—the "secondary effect." Absinthe's herbs contain stimulants that help counteract the depressive effects of alcohol, and anise oils increase circulation, leading to a heightened sense of alertness and lucidity. We find that drinking other liquors is like walking a tightrope, whereas drinking absinthe opens up a nice, wide path. The high is more pronounced, clearer, and comes on much earlier. Call it a placebo if you like.

THE THUJONE CONNECTION

Much of absinthe's psychoactive allure can be traced back to thujone, the neurotoxin found in wormwood, juniper, sage, and mugwort. During the height of absinthe hysteria in the early 1900s, thujone was thought to be a prime culprit in absinthe's poisonous effects. A few grams would be enough to kill a person, but advanced tests from the past few years have shown that pre-ban absinthes actually contained very little thujone—something in the range of three to six milligrams, well below the ten-milligram ceiling set by the Food and Drug Administration in the United States. The occasional absinthe that touts its high levels of thujone probably doesn't have much else to celebrate, and may well be lying to boot. If it's not, all the more reason to avoid it. The unlikely possibility of additional mental stimulation isn't worth the risk.

La Bohème

Light, bubbly, and ready to go—anytime, anywhere.

2 OUNCES LIMONCELLO

1 OUNCE LA FÉE ABSINTH BOHEMIAN

1 OUNCE ORANGE JUICE

4 OUNCES CLUB SODA FLOAT

Shake well and strain over ice. Float club soda.

The Pernodian

———

The Pernodian is about fruit and spice. The rum's cinnamon and Pernod's anise invigorate the orange and coconut flavors.

2 OUNCES PERNOD

1 OUNCE SPICED RUM

1 OUNCE MALIBU RUM

1½ OUNCES ORANGE JUICE

½ OUNCE GRAND MARNIER

Shake well with ice and serve straight up in a tall glass with salted rim. Garnish with an orange wheel.

Furry Navel

———

The Fuzzy Navel grown up. And a little heavier, of course.

1½ OUNCES GRANDE ABSENTE ABSINTHE

1½ OUNCES PEACH SCHNAPPS

3 OUNCES ORANGE JUICE

Build in a tall glass over ice. Garnish with an orange slice.

Furry Framboise

Another take on the Fuzzy Navel, with an assist from the raspberry (framboise in French).

1½ OUNCES LA FÉE ABSINTH BOHEMIAN

1 OUNCE PEACH SCHNAPPS

1 OUNCE CHAMBORD BLACK RASPBERRY LIQUEUR

½ OUNCE RASPBERRY PURÉE

2 OUNCES ORANGE JUICE

Build in a tall glass over ice. Garnish with an orange slice and a raspberry.

YOU KNOW WHAT THIS DRINK NEEDS?
MORE COWBELL

St. George, the first contemporary absinthe legally distilled in the United States, features a monkey holding a cowbell on the label, a bit of a joke after the Alcohol and Tobacco Tax and Trade Bureau rejected its proposed labels more than a dozen times. The cowbell is a sly reference to the *Saturday Night Live* sketch "More Cowbell," where Christopher Walken played music producer Bruce Dickinson recording "(Don't Fear) The Reaper" for Blue Öyster Cult. "More Cowbell" featured Chris Parnell, Chris Kattan, Horatio Sanz, Jimmy Fallon, and Will Ferrell, who so ably wielded the cowbell in question as Gene Frenkle.

Lawn Mower

Made as the Weed Wacker at Tales of the Cocktail in New Orleans. We refined it with a float of St-Germain.

1½ OUNCES CRUZAN SINGLE BARREL RUM

½ OUNCE ST. GEORGE ABSINTHE

1 OUNCE FRESH LEMON JUICE

1 OUNCE PINEAPPLE JUICE

1 DASH PEYCHAUD'S BITTERS

ST-GERMAIN ELDERFLOWER LIQUEUR FLOAT

Shake well and strain over ice. Float St-Germain elderflower liqueur.

YOU SAY LIQUEUR, I SAY LIQUOR

People often mistakenly refer to absinthe as a liqueur, maybe because of anise-based liqueurs like anisette (made with green anise) and pastis (made with star anise). Anise liqueurs have sugar added before bottling and have anywhere from 25 to 45 percent alcohol by volume, whereas absinthes rarely drop below 55 percent.

Sundance Sunset

The official drink of the play-all-day, party-all-night set. Made carefully, the finished drink has red on the bottom, gold in the middle, and a louchey green on top.

4 OUNCES RED BULL

½ OUNCE GRENADINE

1½ OUNCES LE TOURMENT VERT ABSINTHE

Fill a tall glass with ice. Fill three-quarters full with Red Bull (about 4 ounces). Slowly pour about ½ ounce grenadine down the side of the glass so that it settles on the bottom. Float 1½ ounces Tourment to create a layered effect.

Kryptonite

The classic Red Bull and vodka done one better, for long nights in Smallville.

1 OUNCE LUCID ABSINTHE

½ OUNCE KETEL ONE CITROEN

½ OUNCE SOUR APPLE SCHNAPPS

4 OUNCES RED BULL

Build over ice.

MARTINIS
AND SHOTS

You mustn't mind that a poet is a drunk,
rather that drunks are not always poets.

—OSCAR WILDE

The heart of contemporary absinthe, martinis are some of the most imaginative and enjoyable drinks we know of. Many adhere to the Gargoyle's template of absinthe-sugar-acid, with an optional infusion of fruit, but the combinations are endless, and there are enough styles to please everyone. All the martinis are based on a four-ounce pour and can be converted to a shot by halving the recipe. You can substitute simple syrup, rock candy syrup, and blue agave nectar for each other in any recipe, with some subtle variations in the results. Highlights: Gargoyle, La Fée Verte, Poison Apple Martini, Tourment Trance, Senjo.

Gargoyle

Dave Herlong's take on the traditional Lemon Drop, his first absinthe cocktail: "The lemon complements the spice and aromatics of absinthe better than anything I've come across."

2 OUNCES LE TOURMENT VERT ABSINTHE

1 OUNCE ROCK CANDY SYRUP

1 OUNCE SWEET AND SOUR MIX

1 LEMON WEDGE

1 LEMON TWIST

In a mixing tin filled with ice, squeeze the lemon and add the absinthe. Shake very well. Add the rock candy syrup and the sweet and sour. Shake again and strain into a chilled martini glass. (Ice chips and lemon pulp should float.) Garnish with a lemon twist. The finished drink should be a light aqua blue. Consider substituting triple sec for the rock candy syrup for a sharper taste. To make a zestier, more lemon-forward drink, use ½ ounce of simple syrup in place of the rock candy syrup.

*   *   *

The Gargoyle is inarguably the "mother sauce" and has spawned a multitude of variations. Our favorites:

INFERNO: To base ingredients, add two muddled strawberries or purée. Garnish with a strawberry and lemon twist flag.

HAZE: To base ingredients, add six muddled blueberries or purée. Garnish with a blueberry and lemon twist flag.

GRIFFIN: To base ingredients, add six muddled raspberries or purée. Garnish with a raspberry and lemon twist flag.

DOUX FÉE (GENTLE FAIRY): To base ingredients, add 1 ounce pomegranate juice and replace lemon wedge with two lime wedges. Garnish with a lime wheel.

MOULIN ROUGE: With base ingredients mixed and poured in a cocktail glass, drip filtered pomegranate juice down the side of the glass until it separates and creates a layered effect. Garnish with a lemon twist.

THE ABSINTHE ARTISTS

The artists of late-1800s Paris come to us as a group bound by the common thread of absinthe. Given that everyone at the time was drinking absinthe, however, the only unifying element we're left with was their extraordinary creativity, and that came before the green muse. The artists of the day hailed from a range of classes. They were not all Bohemians. Respectability was still a possibility for artists of that period, if they followed the right path. Henri de Toulouse-Lautrec came from a family of aristocrats. Oscar Wilde's father was a surgeon and knight of the British Empire, his mother a prominent poet. Edouard Manet's father was a wealthy and influential judge. Others were destitute and ran away from home at a young age. In addition, the absinthe-connected artists most of us think of as coming from a single generation, like the Rat Pack of the 1960s, were born forty-plus years apart and may have met only in passing, if at all. They're a collective only in hindsight, the ones who bucked convention and accepted stigma, using absinthe as a tool to push creative boundaries where polite society held it strictly in the realm of aperitif.

Charles Baudelaire
Charles Cros
Aleister Crowley
Edgar Degas
Ernest Dowson
Paul Gauguin
Ernest Hemingway
Alfred Jarry
Gustave Kahn
Edouard Manet
Guy de Maupassant

Amedeo Modigliani
Adolphe Monticelli
Alfred de Musset
Pablo Picasso
Raoul Ponchon
Arthur Rimbaud
Henri de Toulouse-Lautrec
Vincent Van Gogh
Paul Verlaine
Oscar Wilde
Emile Zola

Van Gogh

One of the original modern mixed-absinthe cocktails presents in a frothy shade of pink.

2 OUNCES LE TOURMENT VERT ABSINTHE

1¼ OUNCES PINEAPPLE JUICE

¾ OUNCE GRENADINE

1 LEMON WEDGE

Shake well and strain into a chilled cocktail glass. Garnish with a cherry.

VAN GOGH: HIS EAR AND HIS ABSINTHE

Vincent Van Gogh was one of the all-time masters, a prodigy who, with limited formal training, helped define art's Postimpressionist movement and during one fifteen-month stretch in Arles, France, produced a painting, drawing, or watercolor about once a day—each one a masterpiece. But what we really want to know is, why did he cut off his ear? Absinthe?

There's no shortage of theories so intriguing that maybe it's for the best we can't be sure. Mental illness ran in Van Gogh's family, and he may have suffered from depression, schizophrenia, or bipolar disorder. He had recurring seizures; since his death, many doctors have speculated that he had temporal lobe epilepsy, which would have affected his day-to-day personality. He could be physically aggressive, unstable, and obsessed with emotional intimacy, ironically to the point of alienating friends and romantic prospects. Over and over again he failed at these relationships.

After his move to Paris, Van Gogh drank massive amounts of absinthe, even by artists' standards of the day. He often complained of stomach pains, perhaps a symptom of his heavy intake, and was known for his liberal use of yellow, absinthe-tinged tones in his work, best exemplified in *Still Life with Absinthe* (1887). He continued drinking in southern France, where he moved for better light and color, and where he painted *The Night Café* (1888), which depicts the Café de l'Alcazar, an absinthe den in Arles that Van Gogh described as ripe for criminality and madness. Arles had the highest per capita absinthe consumption in France—four times the national average.

The month after he painted *The Night Café*, Van Gogh persuaded Paul Gauguin, another famous absinthe drinker and master Postimpressionist in his own right, to join him in Arles and set up a permanent studio. The union was cursed before it began. Gauguin, sly and manipulative, did not share Van Gogh's idealistic dream and planned to come for a year at most. He stayed an explosive two months. They had long, passionate arguments. Van Gogh had built up the idea of an artists' collective as his creative salvation, and his fear of abandonment might be what drove him to cut. It happened two days before Christmas. The two argued, and Gauguin—had he threatened to leave?—walked out of the house. Much later, he would claim that Van Gogh had followed him while out for a walk and was clutching a razor blade as if to jump him, possibly drunk or in an epileptic fit. Gauguin turned, and Van Gogh instead ran home to cut the lower half of his own left ear.

Van Gogh might not have left the house with a razor blade, or might not have left the house at all before using the blade on himself. But what happened next is clear. He visited a brothel and left the ear with Rachel, a prostitute he knew and whom Gauguin had visited. "Keep this carefully," he told her.

The sequence was not as bizarre as it might seem. Van Gogh

had a masochistic streak and from a young age saw pain and suffering as a way to attract affection from others. Self-mutilation may have been a way to win Gauguin's sympathies and prevent him from leaving. Read differently, the act was simultaneously a self-sacrifice and defiant gesture of victory: in southern France, Van Gogh attended bullfights for the first time and may have internalized the bloody drama, where a winning matador receives one of the bull's ears as a token and then presents it to his female companion or a spectator. Another wrinkle: Jack the Ripper was making sensational headlines at the time. Two months before Van Gogh's ear incident, the serial killer had cut the ears off one of his victims.

The psychological theories are so rich that absinthe hardly seems necessary to explain his behavior. German art historians Hans Kaufmann and Rita Wildegans have even theorized that Van Gogh didn't do it at all and that instead it was Gauguin, a skilled fencer, who either accidentally or intentionally sliced his ear during their argument. Van Gogh didn't seem to think absinthe deserved the blame at least. In October 1889, nine months before he committed suicide, he wrote to his sister Wilhelmina:

> That physician here has been to Paris, and went to see Theo [Van Gogh's brother]; he told [Theo] that he did not consider me a lunatic, but that the crises I have are of an epileptic nature. Consequently alcohol is also not the cause, though it must be understood that it does me no good either. But it is difficult to return to one's ordinary way of life while one is too despondent over the uncertainty of misfortune. And one goes on clinging to the affections of the past.

Red Leather

The name inspired the drink, created for a party of five hundred in the Palms' Hugh Hefner suite. It's all there: the sweet, the tart, the spice, the fruit. Hugh would be proud.

1½ OUNCES LE TOURMENT VERT ABSINTHE

½ OUNCE ABSOLUT VANILIA

1 OUNCE MONIN CHERRY SYRUP

1 OUNCE SWEET AND SOUR MIX

Shake well and strain into a chilled cocktail glass. Garnish with a lemon wedge and a slice of cherry Fruit Roll-Ups.

The Veracruz

Pernod meets tequila as French troops met their Mexican counterparts at the port of Veracruz in 1861, five months before Cinco de Mayo.

2 OUNCES PERNOD

2 OUNCES LA PINTA POMEGRANATE INFUSED TEQUILA

½ OUNCE PURE AGAVE NECTAR

¼ OUNCE HAZELNUT LIQUEUR

Shake well and strain into a chilled cocktail glass with a salted rim. Garnish with an orange wedge.

French Candy Apple

The carnival treat comes off the stick.

2 OUNCES LE TOURMENT VERT ABSINTHE

1 OUNCE SOUR APPLE SCHNAPPS

1 OUNCE APPLE JUICE

1 SPLASH GOLDSCHLÄGER CINNAMON SCHNAPPS

1 SPLASH GRENADINE

Shake well and strain into a chilled cocktail glass. Garnish with an apple slice or a cherry.

*Therefore thus saith the LORD of hosts concerning the prophets;
Behold, I will feed them with wormwood, and make them drink
the water of gall: for from the prophets of Jerusalem is profaneness
gone forth into all the land.*

—JEREMIAH 23:15, KING JAMES BIBLE

ABSINTHE WITHOUT SUGAR?
THE CZECHS TO THE RESCUE

We could hardly have had Belle Époque absinthe without the sugar cube, and, believe it or not, we have the Czech Republic to thank for it. In the mid-1800s, new machines were transforming sugar from a rare luxury good into a middle-class staple. Jakub Krystof Rad managed a processing plant that made candied fruits, sweets, and chocolate in the city of Dacice. At the time, sugar came in large cones or loafs. To use it, you first had to cut it, snip it, or hit it with a hammer. One day in 1841, Jakub's wife, Juliana, was cutting a loaf of sugar while preparing lunch and cut her finger at the same time. She suggested that Jakub begin selling sugar precut in small packages, even going so far as to recommend cutting it into cubes to make it easier to count and stock. Six weeks later, Jakub gave her a lovely anniversary present: a box of 350 sugar cubes—half dyed red and half bleached white. By 1843, he was producing sugar cubes on a mass scale, and the sugar cube has since become one of the world's most widely used Czech inventions.

Twisted Tourment

Light and tropical, the Twisted Tourment is also nice over ice.

1½ OUNCES LE TOURMENT VERT ABSINTHE

1 OUNCE MIDORI MELON LIQUEUR

½ OUNCE PIÑA COLADA MIX

½ OUNCE PINEAPPLE JUICE

½ OUNCE SWEET AND SOUR MIX

Shake well and strain into a chilled cocktail glass. Garnish with a cherry.

Tourment Carnival

Fruity and juicy, a pinkies-up version of the Alabama Slammer.

1 OUNCE LE TOURMENT VERT absinthe

1 OUNCE amaretto

1 OUNCE SOUTHERN COMFORT

⅓ OUNCE COINTREAU orange triple sec liqueur

⅓ OUNCE orange juice

⅓ OUNCE sweet and sour mix

Shake well and strain into a chilled cocktail glass. Garnish with an orange wedge.

The Madagascar

Think tropical abundance, French sophistication, and cruise-ship effervescence—appetites win out over aperitifs.

2 OUNCES PERNOD

2 OUNCES SPRITE

1 OUNCE BANANA SYRUP

½ OUNCE COINTREAU ORANGE TRIPLE SEC LIQUEUR

⅛ OUNCE FRESH LIME JUICE

Shake well and strain into a chilled cocktail glass. Garnish with a lime wheel. Also works—and arguably looks better—as a frozen drink.

La Fée Verte

The third member of the original triumvirate, La Fée Verte twists the Gargoyle's formula yet again. Lime juice makes it more acidic than the Gargoyle or Van Gogh.

2 OUNCES LE TOURMENT VERT ABSINTHE

1½ OUNCES ORANGE JUICE

½ OUNCE ROSE'S SWEETENED LIME JUICE

1 LIME WEDGE

Shake well and strain into a chilled cocktail glass. Squeeze lime wedge and add to glass. Garnish with a lime wheel.

BROKEN DREAMS, BUT NOT FROM ABSINTHE

Critics who faulted absinthe for corrupting Belle Époque society conveniently forgot that many of the most objectionable *absintheurs* had been long in the making, well before tasting absinthe. Paul Verlaine, the vaunted French poet, patronized prostitutes before he was twenty, abused his wife, took up with sixteen-year-old Arthur Rimbaud on the side, and threatened to kill his mother at least twice before breaking three jars in the cupboard in which his mother stored her long-ago-miscarried fetuses. Absinthe played its part, as it did with Van Gogh, but if it had not, surely another alcohol would have taken over the role.

The Impudent

The evil eye and miseries wide,
Said with no thought to slander,
Have given to this fiend of pride
The soul of an old prisoner.

Yes, jettatore, *sad wanderer,*
The first and last of them that sigh,
You dwell in the black shadows where
Men will pursue you till you die.

The children ripen at your look.
Refusals many must you brook.
Since, impudent, your ways annoy.
Beauties that pass, your smiling elves,
Throw not your coins to this bad boy,
But give, instead of alms—yourselves.

—PAUL VERLAINE

Hemingway Revolution

Great with dinner or dessert, the Revolution stars robust red fruits: raspberry, black currant, and cranberry.

1½ ounces La Fée Absinth Bohemian

1½ ounces Chambord black raspberry liqueur

½ ounce raspberry purée

½ ounce crème de cassis

1 splash cranberry juice

Shake well and strain into a chilled cocktail glass. Garnish with a lemon twist.

Le Démon

Falernum (traditionally drank with wormwood bitters) brings touches of almond, lime, and cloves to this version of a Barbados punch.

2 OUNCES PLYMOUTH GIN

1 OUNCE LE TOURMENT VERT ABSINTHE

½ OUNCE VELVET FALERNUM

½ OUNCE FRESH LIME JUICE

Shake well and strain into a chilled cocktail glass. Garnish with a lime wheel.

Absinthe is the aphrodisiac of the self. The green fairy who lives in the absinthe wants your soul. But you are safe with me.
    —GARY OLDMAN AS DRACULA IN *BRAM STOKER'S DRACULA*

Devil's Pearl

A hearty, almost traditional after-dinner drink of herbs, spices, and botanicals.

3 OUNCES KÜBLER ABSINTHE

¼ OUNCE ANISETTE

½ OUNCE SIMPLE SYRUP

1 DASH Angostura BITTERS

1 SPLASH WATER

Shake well and strain into a chilled cocktail glass. Garnish with a lemon twist.

Voodoo Pigalle

Absinthe mixed with Chartreuse was the drink of choice in Belle Époque Pigalle, Paris's red-light district. Midori and lemon lighten up the combo.

2 OUNCES Kübler ABSINTHE

1 OUNCE Midori MELON LIQUEUR

1 OUNCE GREEN Chartreuse

1 LEMON WEDGE

1 SUGAR PACKET

Add squeezed lemon wedge and sugar packet to liquids. Shake well, and strain into a chilled cocktail glass.

THE GREEN FAIRIES:
WOMEN AND ABSINTHE

As absinthe took root with artists in the 1860s, women discovered an unprecedented level of societal tolerance for their absinthe rituals. Just ten years before, the idea of a woman drinking hard alcohol alongside men in cafés would have been *louche* indeed, but culture and mores were changing so fast that women not only were drinking at cafés, they were serving in them too, the brainchild of café owners looking to hustle a few more drinks. For women, drinking absinthe was a gesture of empowerment, like riding a bicycle or, in the 1920s, bobbing their hair.

But it wasn't all Sojourner Truth and Gloria Steinem. A woman could get away with having an absinthe, but her reputation couldn't. Bar-going women were widely regarded as easy, as charity cases, or even as prostitutes. As with opium, women seemed more vulnerable to absinthe addiction than men and often compounded the problem by drinking it undiluted, perhaps to avoid bloat in their corsets. Edgar Degas's *Au Café*, of a beaten-down, isolated-looking woman wearily staring into the middle distance with an absinthe in front of her, became a symbol of the ravages of absinthe on women.

Eden's Apple

———

A lighter version of the Voodoo Pigalle with apple juice and ginger ale.

1 OUNCE KÜBLER ABSINTHE

1 OUNCE MIDORI MELON LIQUEUR

1 OUNCE GREEN CHARTREUSE

½ OUNCE APPLE JUICE

GINGER ALE FLOAT

Shake well and strain into a chilled cocktail glass. Float dry ginger ale.

The breasts of the waitresses of the sailor bars over there, in Genoa or Marseilles, transform any drink; they lean toward the glasses as though siphoned by an invisible jet, something stronger yet than absinthe.

—RAMÓN GÓMEZ DE LA SERNA (*SEINS*), 1917

Green Daiquiri

Hemingway would have approved of this simple daiquiri, even in the Havana days. No rum required.

2 OUNCES ST. GEORGE ABSINTHE

1¼ OUNCES SIMPLE SYRUP

¾ OUNCE FRESH LIME JUICE

Shake well and strain into a chilled cocktail glass. Garnish with a lime wedge.

Poison Apple Martini

Manageable for large groups, this spin on the familiar Apple Martini adds a real kick. Very tasty, very drinkable.

1 OUNCE LE TOURMENT VERT ABSINTHE

1 OUNCE SOUR APPLE SCHNAPPS

1 OUNCE ORANGE JUICE

1 OUNCE SWEET AND SOUR MIX

Shake well and strain into a chilled cocktail glass. Garnish with a cherry. To make the Sundance Film Festival's version of the drink, halve the amount of sour apple schnapps and sweet and sour mix, and add a splash of cranberry juice.

VERMOUTH VS. WORMWOOD

In German, *wermut* means both *vermouth* and *wormwood*. (Try saying *wormwood* with a German accent. See?) Vermouth does contain small amounts of wormwood.

My son, attend unto my wisdom, and bow thine ear to my understanding:

That thou mayest regard discretion, and that thy lips may keep knowledge.

For the lips of a strange woman drop as an honeycomb, and her mouth is smoother than oil:

But her end is bitter as wormwood, sharp as a two-edged sword.

Her feet go down to death; her steps take hold on hell.

—PROVERBS 5:1–5, KING JAMES BIBLE

Absinthe Martini (European Style)

Orange essence and Lucid cozy up in a sweeter yet complex martini.

2 OUNCES MARTINI & ROSSI SWEET VERMOUTH

1 OUNCE LUCID ABSINTHE

1 OUNCE FEE BROTHERS ORANGE BITTERS

Shake well and strain into a chilled cocktail glass. Garnish with an orange slice.

Chameleon

———

Margarita-like at first glance, the Chameleon surprises with a subtle twist of cherry, more fruit and spice than sweet and sour. Perfect with a bag of chips at a summer barbeque.

1½ OUNCES PATRÓN TEQUILA

1 OUNCE LUCID ABSINTHE

1 OUNCE LUXARDO MARASCHINO LIQUEUR

½ OUNCE FRESH LIME JUICE

In a mixing tin filled with ice, add all ingredients and shake well. Strain into a chilled cocktail glass. Garnish with a lime wheel and cherry.

Riverside

Cranberry juice leavens this sweet pink cocktail, a French-Italian collaboration.

1 OUNCE ST. GEORGE ABSINTHE

1 OUNCE LIMONCELLO

1 OUNCE GRAND MARNIER

1 OUNCE CRANBERRY JUICE

Shake well and strain into a chilled cocktail glass. Garnish with a lemon twist.

Le Voûte

Many try to improve on the Manhattan; few succeed. But sample this, with absinthe and hints of orange and cherry, and you'll be putting them away (which is why we call it "The Vault").

2 OUNCES BULLEIT BOURBON

1 OUNCE CINZANO SWEET VERMOUTH

1 OUNCE KÜBLER ABSINTHE

1 SPLASH CLEAR CREEK KIRSCHWASSER CHERRY LIQUEUR

1 SPLASH REGANS' ORANGE BITTERS

Shake well and strain into a chilled cocktail glass. Garnish with an orange slice.

Imperial Morning Glory

The Morning Glory has been around since the 1880s. This version uses Cointreau Noir instead of orange curaçao and real absinthe instead of Prohibition-era pastis.

1 OUNCE COURVOISIER EXCLUSIF

1 OUNCE SAZERAC RYE WHISKEY

2 DASHES ANGOSTURA BITTERS

1 TEASPOON COINTREAU NOIR (ORANGE LIQUEUR/COGNAC BLEND)

1 TEASPOON ROCK CANDY SYRUP

1 TEASPOON KÜBLER ABSINTHE

1 OUNCE CHAMPAGNE FLOAT

Shake well and strain into a chilled cocktail glass. Float Champagne. Garnish with a lemon twist.

The Morning After

With the flowers, with the women,
with absinthe, with fire,
you can divert yourself a little,
playing a role in the plays.
Absinthe drunk on a winter evening,
illuminates the smoky soul in green;
and the flowers on the beloved one
give off a scent before the clear fire.
Then kisses lose their charms,
having lasted a few seasons,
the reciprocal betrayals
have us leave one day without tears.
You burn letters and flowers
and the fire lights our nest
and if the sad life is spared,
only absinthe and hiccups remain.
The portraits are eaten by flames,
the shrivelled fingers are trembling,
you die having slept too long
with the flowers, with the women.

—CHARLES CROS, 1848

Triple French Martini

Grey Goose, Tourment, and Chambord make it triple French.

1 OUNCE GREY GOOSE VODKA

1 OUNCE LE TOURMENT VERT ABSINTHE

1 OUNCE CHAMBORD BLACK RASPBERRY LIQUEUR

1 OUNCE PINEAPPLE JUICE

Shake well and strain into a chilled cocktail glass. Garnish with a lemon twist.

Love That Licorice

This sweet, herbal cocktail, with a creamy texture and hints of chocolate, is ideal as a digestif.

1 OUNCE LUCID ABSINTHE

1 OUNCE SAMBUCA

1 OUNCE WHITE CRÈME DE CACAO

1 OUNCE LIGHT CREAM

In a mixing tin filled with ice, add all ingredients and shake well to mix and help thicken the cream. Strain into a chilled cocktail glass. Garnish with a stick of black licorice.

Hemingway's Dream

The daiquiri meets the mojito in this hybrid harborside cocktail.

2 OUNCES KÜBLER ABSINTHE

2 OUNCES LEMON JUICE

3 CUBES DEMERARA SUGAR

9 MINT LEAVES

Shake well and double strain into a chilled cocktail glass. Garnish with a lemon twist.

Corpse Reviver

A New Orleans classic of magical complexity. Take care not to overwhelm it with absinthe.

1 OUNCE PLYMOUTH GIN

1 OUNCE LILLET BLANC

1 OUNCE GRAND MARNIER

1 OUNCE FRESH LEMON JUICE

2 SPLASHES LUCID ABSINTHE

Shake well and strain into a chilled cocktail glass. Garnish with a lemon twist.

> *The effect, which the absinthe exerts in a direct way on the stom-*
> *ach alone, is highly pernicious. It controls for mischief the natural*
> *power of the stomach to secrete digestive fluid; it interferes with*
> *the solvent power of that fluid itself, so that, taken in what is con-*
> *sidered to be a moderate quantity—a wineglassful or two in the*
> *course of the day—it soon establishes a permanent dyspepsis.*
>
> —FROM THE NEWSPAPER *MANUFACTURER AND BUILDER* (1880)

Green Jaguar

Absinthe replaces the Chartreuse of the standard Jaguar in an
herb-fest of bitters, an off-the-beaten-path throwback.

1½ OUNCES PATRÓN SILVER TEQUILA

¾ OUNCE GRAND MARNIER

¾ OUNCE AMER PICON

¾ OUNCE LUCID ABSINTHE

¼ OUNCE ORANGE JUICE

1 SPLASH REGANS' ORANGE BITTERS

Shake well and strain into a chilled cocktail glass. Garnish with an orange slice.

Obituary Cocktail

A no-frills classic for the absinthe lover created by Gwydion Stone, maker of Marteau absinthe.

2 OUNCES AVIATION GIN

¼ OUNCE MARTINI & ROSSI EXTRA DRY VERMOUTH

¼ OUNCE MARTEAU ABSINTHE

Combine in an iced tumbler. Stir well; strain into a chilled cocktail glass. Garnish with a lemon twist.

Tourment Trance

The signature cocktail of the Palms' Satellite Bar at Moon Nightclub and a Cocktail of the Week in Las Vegas Weekly. *Tart but fruity.*

2 OUNCES LE TOURMENT VERT ABSINTHE

1 OUNCE SOUR APPLE SCHNAPPS

1 OUNCE CRANBERRY JUICE

1 SPLASH GRENADINE

Shake well and strain into a chilled cocktail glass. Garnish with a cherry. The Trance can also be served over ice.

Peppermint Pernod

Peppermint seems made for absinthe, while mango emerges an unconventional companion. Together they make a modern cocktail with a classic feel.

2 OUNCES PERNOD

2 OUNCES FRESH MANGO JUICE

1¼ OUNCES PEPPERMINT SYRUP

Shake well and strain into a cocktail glass. Garnish with a lemon twist.

Shutters on the Pernod

The sweetness of the strawberries is softened by the light herbal qualities of the Pernod, creating the complementary sweet and sour finish.

2 OUNCES PERNOD

2½ OUNCES STRAWBERRY PURÉE

1 OUNCE SWEET AND SOUR MIX

Blend strawberries and sweet and sour together first, then combine with Pernod in a mixing tin, shake well, and strain into a cocktail glass. Garnish with a whole strawberry.

FRANCOPHOBIA

Then as now, a favorite pastime of nineteenth-century Brits was lampooning the decadent and outrageous behavior to be found on the Continent, with Paris as Exhibit A. The popular novelist Marie Corelli, known for her melodramatic, New Agey writing, capitalized on those attitudes in her novel *Wormwood*, a cautionary tale that charts the downfall of the respectable protagonist, Gaston Beauvais, as he gradually descends into addiction, cruelty, and even murder. Stunned after learning of his wife's infidelity, Beauvais sets off down that road when he bumps into the clichéd artist Andre Gessonex, an impoverished friend who paints risqué pictures and suffers "genius without commonsense." Gessonex is famished, and they quickly find their way to a café.

[Gessonex] returned leisurely to his seat opposite me, and I looked at him inquiringly.
"What have you been ordering? A cognac?"
"No."
"What then?"
"Oh, nothing! only—absinthe."
"Absinthe!" I echoed. "Do you like that stuff?"
His eyes opened wide, and flashed a strangely piercing glance at me.
"Like it? I love it! And you?"
"I have never tasted it."
"Never tasted it!" exclaimed Gessonex amazedly. "Mon Dieu! You, a born and bred Parisian, have never tasted absinthe?"

—Marie Corelli (*Wormwood: A Drama of Paris*, 1890)

Absinthe Cocktail

"Cocktail Chronicles" blogger Paul Clarke's take on the absinthe cocktail as it would have been served eighty years ago, give or take.

1 OUNCE MARTEAU ABSINTHE

2 DASHES PEYCHAUD'S BITTERS

2 DASHES BOLS ANISETTE

1 OUNCE CLUB SODA FLOAT

Shake well with ice and strain into a chilled cocktail glass. Float club soda.

A recipe for Insomnia: Bruise a handful of anise seeds, and steep them in waters. Then place in small bags, and bind one bag over each nostril before going to bed.

—C. A. KIRSHTIEN, 1938

75 Shot

Created during World War II and named after a French 75mm cannon. Apple brandy softens the botanicals of the gin and the absinthe.

1 OUNCE CALVADOS APPLE BRANDY
½ OUNCE KÜBLER ABSINTHE
½ OUNCE BOMBAY SAPPHIRE GIN

Shake well and serve in a shot glass.

Absinthe Cleverly

The cousin of the Lemon Drop—the "Orange Drop."

1 OUNCE LUCID ABSINTHE
1 OUNCE GRAND MARNIER

Shake well and serve in a shot glass with a sugared rim.

Senjo

One of our personal favorites tastes more like a Mixed Citrus Drop than a Lemon Drop.

2 OUNCES LE TOURMENT VERT ABSINTHE

1½ OUNCES ROCK CANDY SYRUP

½ OUNCE YUZU (JAPANESE CITRUS JUICE)

In a mixing tin filled with ice, add the absinthe, rock candy syrup, and yuzu. Shake very well and strain into a chilled cocktail glass. Garnish with an orange slice.

Apple Spice Martini

The taste of fall in a glass. Cinnamon, cranberry, apple, vanilla, and lemon create a spice-forward martini.

1 OUNCE LA FÉE ABSINTH BOHEMIAN

1 OUNCE LIMONCELLO

1 OUNCE APPLE CIDER

½ OUNCE ABSOLUT VANILIA

½ OUNCE CRANBERRY JUICE

Shake well and strain into a chilled cocktail glass. Garnish with a cinnamon stick.

ABSINTHE NICKNAMES

La blanche, la bleue, or *clandestine* (clear Swiss absinthe, usually bootlegged)

Une correspondence (short for *une correspondence á Charenton,* "a ticket to Charenton," a famous mental hospital in suburban Paris)

The devil's drink

The fairy with gloomy eyes

The green . . .

. . . ambrosia

. . . curse

. . . fairy (*la fée verte*)

. . . fiend

. . . goddess

. . . menace

... muse
... torment
... witch
King of aperitifs
Madness in a bottle
Opaline
The parrot
Un Pernod (the most popular Belle Époque brand)
The sacred herb (*l'herb sainte*, referring to wormwood)
La verte (French style)

Cinnamon Sidecar

*In this Sidecar, absinthe takes the place of the traditional
brandy. Orange juice hedges the sweet/sour balance.*

1½ OUNCES OBSELLO ABSINTHE

½ OUNCE COINTREAU ORANGE TRIPLE SEC LIQUEUR

½ OUNCE FRESH ORANGE JUICE

1½ OUNCES SWEET AND SOUR MIX

Shake well and strain into chilled cocktail glass. Garnish with
cinnamon sugar on the rim and an orange twist. Make it a cinnamon fig Sidecar by dicing and muddling a Black Mission fig
in a mixing tin and combining with above ingredients. Trade in
the orange twist for a fig slice.

Absinthe makes the tart grow fonder.
—ERNEST DOWSON

Grape Escape

———

Heavy on the fruit but lighter than wine. Can be served with dinner.

1 OUNCE ST. GEORGE ABSINTHE

1 OUNCE ABSOLUT KURANT

1 OUNCE SWEET AND SOUR MIX

½ OUNCE PEACH SCHNAPPS

½ OUNCE CONCORD GRAPE JUICE

10 CONCORD GRAPES (OR ANY PURPLE GRAPES)

In a mixing tin, muddle the grapes and the grape juice. Add ice and all other ingredients. Shake well and double strain into a chilled cocktail glass. Garnish with two frozen grapes.

French Fennel

———

Fresh muddled fennel seeds add a new dimension to this absinthe, while OJ counterbalances.

2 OUNCES GRANDE ABSENTE ABSINTHE

2 OUNCES FRESH ORANGE JUICE

10 FENNEL SEEDS

1 LIME WEDGE

In a mixing tin, muddle the fennel seeds and the lime wedge. Add ice and the remaining ingredients. Shake well and double strain into a chilled cocktail glass. Garnish with a lime wheel.

Indian Summer

A loose interpretation of the pomegranate martini. The cloves bring winter to mind.

2 OUNCES KÜBLER ABSINTHE

1 OUNCE SWEET AND SOUR MIX

1 OUNCE POMEGRANATE JUICE

5 WHOLE CLOVES

In a mixing tin, shake all ingredients well with ice. Strain into a chilled cocktail glass. Garnish with an orange slice.

Autumn Sparkler

Prominent orange flavors, bubbly Champagne, dry absinthe: similar to a mimosa martini.

1½ OUNCES ST. GEORGE ABSINTHE

¾ OUNCE COINTREAU ORANGE TRIPLE SEC LIQUEUR

¾ OUNCE ORANGE CONCENTRATE OR ORANGE JUICE

1 LEMON WEDGE

1 OUNCE CHAMPAGNE FLOAT

In a mixing tin, shake all ingredients well. Strain into a chilled cocktail glass. Float Champagne. Garnish with an orange slice.

ROCKS
DRINKS

*Absinthe is one of the worst enemies of man, and if
we can keep the people of the United States from
becoming slaves to this demon we will do it.*

There's something reassuring and effortless about a rocks glass: the way it fits the curve of your hand, the deceptive heft, the simple charisma. You would expect a glass like that to hold a traditional, no-nonsense drink, and in that spirit we offer recipes that won't disappoint, like the Sazerac, the Flip, and the Frappé. But we'd be remiss if we didn't also direct you to some modern creations as well, drinks at home in the modern bar but with the gravitas to comfortably fill a rocks glass. Each drink is based on a roughly three-ounce pour and may or may not contain actual ice. Highlights: Scottish Licorice, Warm & Toasty.

Absinthe Sazerac

———

One of our oldest cocktails, the toast of New Orleans, is where it all began for American absinthe.

1½ OUNCES SAZERAC RYE

3 DROPS PEYCHAUD'S BITTERS

½ OUNCE ROCK CANDY SYRUP

3 DROPS LUCID ABSINTHE

Add rye, bitters, and rock candy syrup to a cocktail shaker with a few ice cubes. Shake gently or stir. Pour the drops of absinthe into a chilled rocks glass and swirl around to coat the inside of the glass. Pour out any excess. Strain the rye mixture into the seasoned glass and twist a lemon peel over the glass to release the essential oils.

THE SAZERAC

Various drink guides cite the Sazerac as the first cocktail, or first American cocktail, though there's no reliable evidence of that. What the Sazerac undoubtedly is, is one of New Orleans's oldest and most revered drinks. Bartenders anywhere else most likely would look at you slack-jawed if you were to ask for a Sazerac—even more so before the absinthe ban was lifted.

That's not the case in New Orleans, where it never really went out of style. Some say it was invented by Antoine Amadie Peychaud, a Creole apothecary and the man behind Peychaud's bitters, but that's more legend than history. The drink dates to the late eighteenth century, when Peychaud would have been a small child. More likely his bitters complemented Sazeracs handsomely, and in time he came to receive full credit.

Reverence and tradition have not prevented bartenders from fiddling with the recipe. The original used cognac instead of rye. Some use bourbon, though rye still makes for the best mix. The classic Sazerac calls for only a few drops of absinthe—just enough to coat the glass—but you could get away with using a little extra. Excess, of course, is also a New Orleans tradition.

Lemonilla

A spicy little cocktail that's straight to the point—a vanilla Lemon Drop mixed with 138-proof absinthe. A good after-dinner drink.

1 OUNCE GRANDE ABSENTE absinthe

1 OUNCE LIMONCELLO

1 OUNCE ABSOLUT VANILIA

Build over ice in a rocks glass.

LE RIVIÈRE VERTE

By 1900, the absinthe distiller Pernod Fils (Pernod and Sons) was one of the largest and most successful companies in France and a pioneer in the humane and enlightened treatment of its mostly female workers. Pernod Fils offered profit sharing, unemployment, and a pension plan that insured its workers against accidents. The company boasted day care, schools, and medical benefits at a time when most companies exploited their workers mercilessly.

Lightning struck the Pernod distillery in Pontarlier, France, on August 11, 1901, and started a devastating fire. The damage would have been much worse if not for a resourceful employee who emptied the vats of flammable absinthe into the drains, which ran directly into the Doubs River next to the plant. The river *louched* like a glass of Pernod and smelled of anise for miles downstream. Firefighters on the scene could cool off by dipping their helmets into the river and drinking for free—much appreciated since it took four days to put out the fire.

Pernod was at the height of its powers then and invested heavily in new state-of-the-art equipment that in a way put the company in a better position than it was before. For the region's residents, the fire was more of a toss-up. The spilled absinthe, curiously, showed up in the Loue River, a tributary of the Doubs on the other side of the Jura Mountains. Nine years later, E. A. Martel, the father of modern cave science, used dye tracing to confirm that the Doubs actually loses some of its water to the Loue through a spring that runs under the mountains. Angry mill owners along the Doubs began using conrete to plug swallow holes in the river that they correctly presumed allowed water to escape to the Loue. Soon, of course, Loue Valley residents were also missing water. A court finally had to intervene on behalf of the Loue Valley; new plugs on the Doubs would be illegal, but the court allowed concrete already in place to remain.

Rosemary Daisy

Absinthe is at its best in herbal concoctions, and rosemary heeds the call.

1¼ OUNCES OBSELLO ABSINTHE

1¼ OUNCES KETEL ONE CITROEN VODKA

½ OUNCE SWEET AND SOUR MIX

1 SPRIG ROSEMARY

1 LEMON WEDGE

In a mixing tin, muddle the rosemary sprig and lemon wedge. Add ice, absinthe, vodka, and sweet and sour. Shake well. Double strain into a rocks glass filled with ice and garnish with a second sprig of rosemary and a lemon twist.

Scottish Licorice

A sipping drink, perfect for the fireside or as an after-dinner cocktail. Scotch and Drambuie alone would make a Rusty Nail. Here the Kübler visibly louches and adds a strong anise flavor Scotch drinkers should enjoy.

2 OUNCES KÜBLER ABSINTHE

1 OUNCE DRAMBUIE

1 OUNCE TWELVE-YEAR SINGLE-MALT SCOTCH

Shake well and add to a chilled rocks glass with ice. Garnish with a lemon twist. If you pour a sweetened absinthe or prefer a sharper taste, consider adding less Drambuie.

French Alexander

A variation on the traditional Brandy Alexander with an all-French lineup.

1 OUNCE COURVOISIER EXCLUSIF

1 OUNCE GODIVA MILK CHOCOLATE LIQUEUR

1 OUNCE HALF AND HALF

1 SPLASH LE TOURMENT VERT ABSINTHE

Shake well and strain into a rocks glass.

Flavorpill Orange Fresh

A low-carb cocktail developed for Flavorpill, a national network of city guides.

1 OUNCE LE TOURMENT VERT ABSINTHE

JUICE OF 2 ORANGE WEDGES

2 OUNCES CLUB SODA FLOAT

Shake well and roll into a rocks glass. Float club soda. Garnish with an orange wedge.

THE ABSINTHE MURDERS

At the dawn of the twentieth century, as many forces aligned against absinthe as had worked in its favor fifty years earlier. Promoters of progressive social causes like the temperance movement, workers' rights, and food safety took heart in the reforms being instituted and came to see absinthe as a major problem to be solved. In 1900, France consumed more alcohol per capita than any other country in the world, and among aperitifs absinthe accounted for 90 percent of consumption. As the medical establishment spoke out about the dangers of absinthe, the murder case of Jean Lanfray, a vineyard worker who had killed his wife and two young daughters, seized the newspaper headlines.

In the dog days of summer 1905, Lanfray argued with his wife about his not having milked the cows and her not having polished his boots. He had had more than a dozen drinks, and he opened fire with a rifle, first on her, then on their four-year-old daughter, Rose, then on their two-year-old daughter, Blanche. He had the entire country's attention. Two of his drinks had been absinthes, and given the widespread ill will toward the drink, papers began calling the killings the "absinthe murders." At the trial, Lanfray's lawyers used an "absinthe madness" defense, claiming he couldn't be held responsible for his mental state during the murders. A jury sentenced Lanfray to prison for thirty years for four murders—his wife had been four months' pregnant—but he hung himself three days later. Absinthe's days, too, were numbered.

Absinthe Spritzer

The spritzer, tasty in its own right, is also a blank canvas for the DIYer.

1 OUNCE LE TOURMENT VERT ABSINTHE

JUICE OF 2 LEMON WEDGES

2 OUNCES CLUB SODA FLOAT

Shake well and roll into a rocks glass. Float club soda. Garnish with a lemon wedge. Or dress it up with an ounce of cherry liqueur, pineapple juice, or grenadine, or a half ounce of Cointreau or triple sec.

And what am I? My dear friends, I have told you,—an absintheur! . . . I am a thing more abject than the lowest beggar that crawls through Paris whining for a soul!—I am a slinking, shuffling beast, half monkey, half man, whose aspect is so vile, whose body is so shaken with delirium, whose eyes are so murderous, that if you met me by chance in the day-time you would probably shriek for sheer alarm! But you will not see me thus—daylight and I are not friends. I have become like a bat or an owl in my hatred of the sun! . . . For twenty francs, you can purchase me body and soul,—for twenty francs I will murder or steal,—all true absintheurs are purchasable!

—MARIE CORELLI (*WORMWOOD: A DRAMA OF PARIS*, 1890)

ABSINTHE BANS BY YEAR

1898	Belgian Congo
1906	Belgium, Brazil
1908	Holland
1910	Switzerland
1912	Canada, United States
1914	Morocco
1915	France
1923	Germany

Absinthe Flip

Makeable at most any bar and just as easy to sip, the Flip is really a short, loose interpretation of a Margarita.

1 OUNCE ST. GEORGE ABSINTHE

1 OUNCE COINTREAU ORANGE TRIPLE SEC LIQUEUR

1 OUNCE SWEET AND SOUR MIX

Shake well and strain into a chilled cocktail glass.

Absinthe Frappé

Simple frappés traditionally get diluted with water, but we say use what suits you and make your flavor.

2 OUNCES ST. GEORGE ABSINTHE

1 OUNCE FLAVORING OF YOUR CHOICE—GRENADINE, LIME JUICE, ELDERFLOWER, LEMON JUICE, CHAMBORD, PINEAPPLE JUICE, APPLE JUICE, ETC.

Build over crushed ice in a rocks glass.

Absinthe Frappé

It will free you first from the burning thirst
That is born of a night of the bowl,
Like a sun 'twill rise through the inky skies
That so heavily hang o'er your soul.
At the first cool sip on your fevered lip
You determine to live through the day,
Life's again worth while as with dawning smile
You imbibe your absinthe frappé.
—LYRICS BY GLENN MACDONOUGH, 1906
(FROM THE OPERETTA *IT HAPPENED IN NORDLAND*)

Warm & Toasty

An iced drink, curiously fragrant and citrusy, that nevertheless fulfills the name's promise.

1½ OUNCES LE TOURMENT VERT ABSINTHE

1½ OUNCES GRAND MARNIER

Build in a large snifter and add ice. Garnish with an orange twist zested into the glass.

Absinth: *Ultra-violent poison: one glass and you're dead. Journalists drink it while writing their articles. Has killed more soldiers than the Bedouins.*

—GUSTAV FLAUBERT IN THE SARDONIC "DICTIONARY OF ACCEPTED IDEAS," POSTHUMOUSLY PUBLISHED IN 1911

Bella Frappé

Deceptively simple, light, and bubbly—something like a raspberry absinthe Margarita.

1 OUNCE OBSELLO ABSINTHE

¾ OUNCE COINTREAU ORANGE TRIPLE SEC LIQUEUR

5 FRESH RASPBERRIES

JUICE OF HALF A LIME

1 SPLASH SIMPLE SYRUP

4 OUNCES CHAMPAGNE

Muddle berries with lime juice and simple syrup. Fill with ice and add absinthe and Cointreau and shake. Strain into tall glass over ice. Fill with Champagne. Garnish with fresh raspberries.

French Derby

We horse-traded with the Brown Derby: absinthe instead of bourbon, orange instead of grapefruit. A bit of rosemary, and you're off to the races.

2 OUNCES LUCID ABSINTHE

1 OUNCE HONEY-ROSEMARY SYRUP

3 ORANGE SLICES

In a rocks glass, muddle oranges and honey-rosemary syrup. Fill with ice and add absinthe. Garnish with a rosemary sprig. (Making the syrup is easy: Heat 1 cup honey and ½ cup water with 3–4 sprigs of rosemary, stirring until well incorporated. Let cool; strain out rosemary.)

ALEISTER CROWLEY CARRIES THE TORCH

Just as absinthe was fading as an institution, an ambassador arrived to pick up its mantle of mysticism more enthusiastically than any of the French artists and poets had a generation before. The British mystic, yogi, and author Aleister Crowley was cantankerous, crude, funny, and supremely self-regarding. One of his most famous works is an essay called "Absinthe: The Green Goddess" that he wrote in one sitting in 1917 while waiting for a woman friend to meet him at the Old Absinthe House on Bourbon Street in New Orleans.

The Old Absinthe House is ground zero for American absinthe and has been since 1874, and the chance union of writer and subject produced one of the great ban-era works on absinthe. In it Crowley invites us to a chair at his elbow to imagine a time we could not otherwise know. Three years after he visited, the bar and fountains at the Old Absinthe House were removed overnight and stashed in a warehouse on Bourbon Street to prevent agents of Prohibition from destroying them in order to send a message. The original bar and fountains didn't return until 2004 as part of a major historical renovation.

"The Green Goddess" is grandiose and meandering, but it's also entertaining, and we've distilled a small portion, drawn from three-quarters of the way through the essay, to give you a little taste:

The Old Absinthe House is not a place. It is not bounded by four walls. It is headquarters to an army of philosophies. . . . It is as if the first diviner of absinthe had been indeed a magician intent upon a combination of sacred drugs which should cleanse, fortify and perfume the human soul. . . .

Let then the pilgrim enter reverently the shrine, and drink his absinthe as a stirrup-cup; for in the right conception of this life as an ordeal of chivalry lies the foundation of every perfection of philosophy. "Whatsoever ye do, whether ye eat or drink, do all to the glory of God!" applies with singular force to the absintheur. So may he come victorious from the battle of life to be received with tender kisses by some green-robed archangel, and crowned with mystic vervain in the Emerald Gateway of the Golden City of God.

DECADENT CONCOCTIONS

CHAMPAGNE, FROZEN, ALCHEMY, JULEPS

*One cup of [absinthe] took the place of the evening
papers, of all the old evenings in cafés . . . of all
things he had enjoyed and forgotten and that
came back to him when he tasted that opaque,
bitter, tongue-numbing, brain-warming,
stomach-warming, idea-changing liquid alchemy.*

—ERNEST HEMINGWAY,

FOR WHOM THE BELL TOLLS

In the popular imagination, Belle Époque absinthe drinkers were either criminal maniacs or self-indulgent artistes awash in decadence. Both assumptions shoot wide of the mark, but the decadent label may have fit better than the criminal one. "Paris has long been playing a losing game," the novelist Marie Corelli wrote in 1900. "Her men are dissolute,—her women shameless—her youth of both sexes depraved,—her laws are corrupt—her arts decadent—her religion dead." So let's say for the sake of argument that the French were a bit decadent. If they had the option, wouldn't they have chosen to dress up their aperitifs with something more than sugar? We think they would. Highlights: Floral-Scented Bubbles, Absinthe Caviar, Lava Lamp.

Champagne Cocktails

Absinthe Champagne Cocktail

Absinthe lends the Champagne cocktail an almost iridescent appearance.

1 SUGAR CUBE

½ OUNCE KÜBLER ABSINTHE

4 OUNCES PERRIER-JOUËT CHAMPAGNE

In a Champagne flute, soak the sugar cube in absinthe. Fill glass with Champagne, stir, and garnish with a lemon twist.

"Do you have any real absinthe?" Roger asked the bar waiter.

"It's not supposed to be," the waiter said. "But I have some."

"The real Couvet Pontarlier sixty-eighth degree? Not the Tarragova?"

"Yes, sir," the waiter said. "I can't bring you the bottle. It will be in an ordinary Pernod bottle."

"I can tell it," Roger said.

—ERNEST HEMINGWAY ("THE STRANGE COUNTRY")

Sonnet de l'Absinthe

Absinthe, I adore you truly!
It seems, when I drink you,
I breathe in the young forest's soul,
During the beautiful green season!
Your perfume disconcerts me
And in your opal color
I see the heavens of yore
As through an open door.

What does it matter, O refuse of the cursed!
That you be a vain paradise,
So long as you satisfy my vice;
And if, before I enter the door,
You make me put up with life,
By acquainting me with death.

—RAOUL PONCHON, 1886

Death in the Afternoon

The classic Hemingway cocktail immortalized in his eponymous novel on bullfighting in Spain.

½ OUNCE LA FÉE ABSINTHE PARISIENNE
4½ OUNCES PERRIER-JOUËT CHAMPAGNE

Stir together in a Champagne flute.

Mind-Altering Mimosa

Absinthe's secondary effect is a natural for this essential morning cocktail.

½ OUNCE LUCID ABSINTHE

1 OUNCE FRESH ORANGE JUICE

3½ OUNCES PERRIER-JOUËT CHAMPAGNE

Stir together in a Champagne flute.

Mad Mango Mimosa

Much less acidic than the OJ-based variety, and more effervescent.

½ OUNCE LA FÉE ABSINTHE PARISIENNE

1 OUNCE MANGO PURÉE

3½ OUNCES PERRIER-JOUËT CHAMPAGNE

In a mixing tin filled with ice, add the absinthe and the mango purée and stir well to incorporate. Strain into a Champagne flute and fill with Champagne. Stir.

Floral-Scented Bubbles

Here sugar and absinthe replace the traditional bitters of a Champagne cocktail, and the elderflower adds a sweet, floral essence. Enjoy it before dinner or with appetizers, shellfish, and cheese platters.

½ OUNCE KÜBLER ABSINTHE

½ OUNCE ST-GERMAIN ELDERFLOWER LIQUEUR

1 SUGAR CUBE

4 OUNCES PERRIER-JOUËT CHAMPAGNE

In a mixing tin filled with ice, add the absinthe and liqueur. Let it sit for a minute, just long enough to chill, and then give it a little stir. Strain it into a Champagne flute, add the sugar cube, and fill with Champagne. Garnish with a lemon twist.

Fuzzy French Bellini

———

A zestier version of the subtle, staid Bellini.

½ OUNCE OBSELLO ABSINTHE
1 OUNCE WHITE PEACH PURÉE (PEELED)
3½ OUNCES PERRIER-JOUËT CHAMPAGNE

Stir together in a Champagne flute.

Razzle Dazzle

———

Cousin to the Kir Royale. Raspberry brings the razzle, Champagne brings the dazzle.

½ OUNCE LA FÉE ABSINTH BOHEMIAN
1 OUNCE RASPBERRY PURÉE
3½ OUNCES PERRIER-JOUËT CHAMPAGNE

Stir together in a Champagne flute.

Absinthe Royale

Another take on the Kir Royale, this one with a black currant flavor and a regal purple color.

½ OUNCE LUCID ABSINTHE

½ OUNCE CRÈME DE CASSIS

4 OUNCES PERRIER-JOUËT CHAMPAGNE

Stir together in a Champagne flute and garnish with a lemon twist.

Paris Lights

A lighter, more refined absinthe sour.

1 OUNCE GRANDE ABSENTE ABSINTHE

1 OUNCE SWEET AND SOUR MIX

3½ OUNCES PERRIER-JOUËT CHAMPAGNE

½ OUNCE ST-GERMAIN ELDERFLOWER LIQUEUR FLOAT

Stir together in a tall glass with ice. Float St-Germain elderflower liqueur.

Frozen Cocktails

Frozen Absinthe Mimosa

Schnapps and absinthe lend some complexity to the traditional mimosa. We recommend taking it poolside.

2 OUNCES ST. GEORGE ABSINTHE

1 OUNCE PEACH SCHNAPPS

3 OUNCES ORANGE JUICE CONCENTRATE

3 OUNCES PERRIER-JOUËT CHAMPAGNE

Blend with shaved ice. Pour into a 14-ounce glass. Top with Champagne, and garnish with an orange slice.

White Fairy Fusion

Absinthe takes the place of Bacardi 151 in this version of the Miami Vice.

1½ OUNCES LE TOURMENT VERT ABSINTHE

¾ OUNCE MALIBU RUM

6 OUNCES ISLAND OASIS PIÑA COLADA MIXER

1 OUNCE ISLAND OASIS STRAWBERRY MIXER

Blend with shaved ice. Pour Island Oasis strawberry mixer into bottom of empty 14-ounce glass. Pour blended mixture on top of strawberry mix in glass. Garnish with a pineapple slice and a strawberry.

Merry Fairy

As fruity and tropical as you can get and perfect for a poolside party. Absinthe adds body but doesn't define the cocktail.

1½ OUNCES ST. GEORGE ABSINTHE

¾ OUNCE AMARETTO

3 OUNCES ISLAND OASIS LEMONADE MIXER

3 OUNCES FRESH PINEAPPLE JUICE

½ OUNCE GRENADINE FLOAT

½ OUNCE MIDORI FLOAT

Blend with shaved ice. Float first with grenadine and then Midori for a layered red-and-green effect. Garnish with a lemon wedge and a cherry.

STARRY NIGHT

After the reactor explosion at Chernobyl in 1986, Soviet citizens buzzed about a Bible passage, Revelation 8:10–11 ("The Seventh Seal") that seemed to foretell the disaster. It describes a great star named Wormwood falling from the sky, "burning as a torch," that polluted a river and killed many people with its bitter poison. Some noted that a Ukrainian translation of wormwood is *chornobyl*. But *chornobyl* more accurately refers to mugwort, a wormwood cousin. The Ukrainian term for wormwood is *polyn hirkyy*.

Green Devil

The Green Devil is a brisk, two-level cocktail of pineapple and melon: a green base of Midori and a white top layer of juice and liquor.

1½ OUNCES LE TOURMENT VERT ABSINTHE

¾ OUNCE MALIBU RUM

3 OUNCES ISLAND OASIS PIÑA COLADA MIXER

3 OUNCES FRESH PINEAPPLE JUICE

1 OUNCE MIDORI MELON LIQUEUR

Blend the absinthe, rum, piña colada, and pineapple juice with shaved ice. Pour the Midori into the bottom of a 14-ounce glass and add the blended mixture on top. The two layers will bleed together in the glass. Garnish with a cherry.

Tourment Tsunami

———

Created for poolside sipping, the Tsunami sports a Solomonic balance of sweetness and acidity.

2 OUNCES LE TOURMENT VERT ABSINTHE

½ OUNCE YUZU (JAPANESE CITRUS JUICE)

5 OUNCES ISLAND OASIS LEMONADE MIXER

1 OUNCE ISLAND OASIS STRAWBERRY MIXER

Blend with shaved ice. Pour into a 14-ounce glass. Garnish with a lemon wedge.

Tourment Tidal Wave

———

The Tidal Wave is a variation of the vodka-based frozen electric lemonade, but one that's looser and with more robust flavor. And it looks great at the beach.

2 OUNCES LE TOURMENT VERT ABSINTHE

1 OUNCE BLUE CURAÇAO

6 OUNCES ISLAND OASIS LEMONADE MIXER

Blend with shaved ice. Pour into a 14-ounce glass. Garnish with a lemon wedge.

Absinthe Suissesse

Sweet and frothy, the Suissesse has long been favored as a breakfast cocktail in France and New Orleans.

1½ OUNCES KÜBLER ABSINTHE

½ OUNCE ORGEAT SYRUP

1 EGG WHITE

½ OUNCE HEAVY CREAM

Combine all ingredients in a blender with shaved ice and flash-blend for five seconds. Serve in a chilled cocktail glass. For less fat (but also less froth), replace the heavy cream with whipping cream or light cream.

I remember a girl I knew in my bachelor days. An American, she had worked as a model in several haute couture salons in Paris and . . . asked me if I would like to have a martini as a nightcap. . . . She stirred up a pitcher of martinis and brought it on a tray with glasses and a bottle of absinthe. . . .

    As for the morning after . . . The Suissesse is regarded by many as one of the finest hangover cures known to man.

            —MAURICE ZOLOTOW (*PLAYBOY*, 1971)

Alchemy

Fairy on Fire

Proceed with caution. This one, like the Flaming Dr Pepper it's modeled after, can sneak up on you.

1½ OUNCES AMARETTO

½ OUNCE LA FÉE ABSINTH BOHEMIAN

1 (12-OUNCE) CAN RED BULL

Pour the amaretto into a shot glass and float the absinthe on top. Carefully light the absinthe, drop the shot into a pint glass half full of cold Red Bull, and shoot it.

BURNING QUESTIONS

The movie *Moulin Rouge!* showed absinthe drinkers at the café lighting their drinks on fire; the process involves soaking a sugar cube with absinthe atop the absinthe spoon and lighting it, then letting it burn down and adding water. Burning doesn't affect the taste, and bars looking to inject a little more flair into their presentation often set the absinthe on fire. It doesn't hurt anything as long as you're careful, but it's a stunt that came out of the Czech Republic in the early 1990s. Movie directors who show it as a nineteenth-century French ritual are taking historical liberties and, moreover, are playing with fire.

Cottontail

In honor of Hugh Hefner, who knows the power of an image.

1 OUNCE LIMONCELLO

1 LEMON WEDGE

1 PALM-SIZED BALL OF COTTON CANDY, BLUE OR PINK

1¾ OUNCES LE TOURMENT VERT ABSINTHE

6 OUNCES LEMON SODA

In a large cocktail goblet (piña colada glass), add Limoncello and squeeze the lemon wedge. Fill glass with cubed ice almost to the top. Place the cotton candy in a ball over the rim of the glass, taking care not to let it touch the ice. Add a large straw if you wish. Pour the absinthe over the cotton candy; the drink will take on the color of the melted cotton candy. Add the soda, stir, and serve. Ideal as a tableside drink for parties where guests can pour their own absinthe and soda to complete the drink.

Absinthe Caviar

The prince of party tricks. Make it with plain gelatin or create a custom flavor (see below).

8 OUNCES LE TOURMENT VERT ABSINTHE

5 SHEETS OF GELATIN

Proof the gelatin in cool water until soft and slippery. Add it to the warmed absinthe and stir until dissolved. (You can create a custom "caviar" flavor by adding a liqueur such as grenadine or juice—pomegranate, lemon, raspberry, blood orange—to the absinthe before mixing with the gelatin. You can even add sugar or mixers, as long as you maintain the right proportions of liquid to gelatin.) Transfer to a squeeze bottle and cool in refrigerator. Meanwhile, place a large container of canola oil in the freezer until almost frozen. When it's ready, remove from freezer and slowly and carefully drip the gelatin absinthe into the oil to create tiny balls of caviar. Let the mixture sit in the freezer for about 30 minutes before straining out the caviar. Rinse with *ice-cold water* to remove as much oil as possible. Transfer caviar to a clean towel to remove any remaining oil. We serve them on sugar-coated citrus triangles at parties.

Lava Lamp

Absinthe Caviar + Champagne = the ultimate delicacy. Dry Champagnes will contrast better with sweet flavored gelatins.

4 OUNCES CHAMPAGNE

1 TABLESPOON ABSINTHE CAVIAR (PAGE 123)

Add caviar to the Champagne and watch as it bobs up and down with the bubbles.

Juleps

Tourmented Mint Julep

---

*Tourment's strong mint flavors add a new dimension to the
classic mint julep, normally made with bourbon. To further
the sacrilege, add raspberry purée or muddled berries to make
a Tourmented Raspberry Mint Julep.*

2½ OUNCES LE TOURMENT VERT ABSINTHE

1 OUNCE SIMPLE SYRUP

1 LARGE SPRIG OF MINT (ABOUT 8 LEAVES)

Place the simple syrup and 1 mint sprig in a mixing tin and
gently bruise the mint leaves, taking care not to tear them. Add
the absinthe and swirl the tin to disperse the mint oil. (For a
Raspberry Mint Julep, add 1 ounce raspberry purée or 10 fresh,
muddled berries with the syrup and absinthe.) Strain this
mixture into a silver julep chalice filled to the top with crushed
ice. (The chalice will stay cold longer than a bar glass; alternatively, you can keep the glasses frozen before serving.) With a
bar spoon, stir this mixture until well integrated and very cold.
Top off with more crushed ice. Garnish with a second sprig of
mint and lightly dust with powdered sugar.

PAUL NATHAN GETS BUSTED

Who hasn't adopted a "better to ask forgiveness than permission" attitude toward nonsensical laws from time to time, especially when the incentive to skirt them was strong and the likelihood of paying the piper remote? Nathan found himself in just such a situation a few years back when he got too evangelical about illegal absinthe. He discovered the piper wasn't as remote as he thought.

Back in the 1990s, when the only practical way for Americans to get absinthe was to buy online, I began traveling to Europe to perform magic and, in my downtime, sought out absinthes I never would have been able to find in San Francisco. Over a span of years, I got the chance to sample hundreds of absinthes in Spain, England, Germany, and elsewhere. Naturally, I didn't go on enough benders to finish all those bottles myself, and a few found their way back home with me. More than a few.

The more I tasted, the more enthusiastic I grew, and I couldn't resist evangelizing a little. Even then, an inexpensive bottle fetched a handsome price, and what if you splurged on an Internet order only to have Customs seize your stuff or discover after one sip that you hated it? A close-knit tribe coalesced around my European discoveries.

One thing led to another, and in 2003, I threw my first bona fide absinthe party at my theater with live music, a midnight cabaret, absinthe-inspired Impressionist art, and more than thirty brands of absinthe gathered from my travels. A crack team of bartenders spent a week before the event sampling absinthe and learning how to pour. Absinthe's time-consuming ritual, I've found, makes extra bartenders a must when serving absinthe. Plus, guests understandably had questions: What is it? Is it safe? What brand or recipe will I like? We gathered answers as best as we could, expecting maybe fifty people. Two hundred showed up. Barnaby Conrad, the author of Absinthe: History in a Bottle, came and signed copies of his book. It was, in short, a great party.

It was also completely illegal. My lawyer says I was breaking more than thirty different state, federal, and international laws, not least of which was that absinthe was banned for human consumption. I decided to make absinthe parties a quarterly affair. If you lived in San Francisco and were interested in absinthe, you probably knew about them. They were never secret—no back entrances or passwords. As word spread, attendance jumped. It was inevitable we would get busted.

It all went down at a party a couple of days before New Year's Eve in 2006. Several people had turned up who made the doorman suspicious. They looked like cops, he thought. As it was a private party, he sent them away. A half hour later, they came back, this time in full SWAT gear. They charged the gate and forced their way in as our security guard tried to shut it. My best bartender was a girl named Cat. An officer caught her with a bottle in one hand and cash in the other. When he grabbed her wrist and asked what was in the bottle, she gave him a knowing smile. She thought someone had hired a male stripper.

Alas, this was no fantasy. There really was no talking our way out of it. I stayed until five in the morning while officers inventoried my liquor, money, and supplies and then confiscated it all, including more than a hundred bottles of my favorite beverage. Five of us were cited and released. It was one of the largest alcohol busts in modern California history and the only absinthe bust in modern times. The police were professional and gracious, so much so that when my four accomplices and I showed up in court, we found the district attorney had not filed any charges against us. We were free to go—no fine, no probation.

Given that they hadn't charged us, it struck me as unfair

that the government should confiscate my property. I called the California Department of Alcoholic Beverage Control (ABC). Officials there congratulated me on not being charged. I told them I wanted my absinthe back.

A long silence followed. "That's going to be a problem," they said.

I pressed, pointing out that it is not illegal to possess absinthe—only to sell it. Since I had not been convicted of selling, there really was no reason for them not to give it back. The ABC researched the issue for six months and ultimately conceded the point. They could find nothing on the books in California that outlawed the possession of absinthe.

For years, decades even, American laws regarding absinthe have been inscrutable. We talk about a lifting of "the ban," but it's difficult to say when and to what extent absinthe became legal. Over time, several rules and regulations were revised that essentially unlocked the door to legal absinthe, but no one had thought to try the knob. The change was so obscure and back-channel that not even the US government realized that absinthe was legal until 2007. As of this printing, there are more than twenty brands of absinthe available in the United States. Someday the brands available will number in the hundreds, proof that modern absinthe is no mere trend, and it will take its rightful place alongside liquors like gin, vodka, and rum as a bar staple. When that day comes, we'll all meet up and throw back a few absinthe cocktails together—this time secure in our place on the right side of the law.

HOT DRINKS
AND PUNCHES

*It is at Brussels that they consume the most brandy,
at Madrid the most chocolate, at Amsterdam the most
gin, at London the most wine, at Constantinople the
most coffee, at Paris the most absinthe; those are all
the useful notions. Paris takes the palm on the whole.*

—VICTOR HUGO, *LES MISÉRABLES*

We think of absinthe as a crisp, refreshing drink, but it more than makes itself at home in hot cocktails too. Thank the plant-based flavonoids, which mimic tannins that dry the mouth and make brandies, scotches, bourbons, and wines such attractive base spirits for hot drinks. The same hot–cold duality recommends absinthe for any number of punches. When mixing hot drinks, wait a beat or two between the stir and the vigorous inhale, or you could find yourself huffing fumes. Highlights: Hazel Café, Tourment Toddy, Hot Spiced Cranberry.

Hot Drinks

Hazel Café

The flavors of light anise and hazelnut could depose Irish Coffee and Mexican Coffee as the kings of after-dinner libations.

6 OUNCES HOT, STRONG COFFEE

1½ OUNCES PERNOD

½ OUNCE FRANGELICO HAZELNUT LIQUEUR

In a large ceramic or porcelain mug, add ingredients in order and stir well.

French Press

———

Same as an Irish coffee, but with Tourment rather than Jameson's.

5 OUNCES HOT, STRONG, FRENCH PRESS COFFEE

1½ OUNCES LE TOURMENT VERT ABSINTHE

1 SUGAR CUBE

In a large ceramic or porcelain mug, add ingredients in order and stir well.

French Café

———

After-dinner coffees can easily become bloated with too much alcohol and too many sweeteners, but the French Café is a fine example of effective, and unusual, simplicity.

5 OUNCES HOT, STRONG COFFEE

1 OUNCE LE TOURMENT VERT ABSINTHE

1 OUNCE GRAND MARNIER

1 SUGAR CUBE

In a large ceramic or porcelain mug, add ingredients in order and stir well.

Le Grande Café

Le Grande, with its chocolate liqueur and nutty Frangelico, can almost take the place of dessert.

5 OUNCES HOT, STRONG COFFEE

½ OUNCE GRANDE ABSENTE ABSINTHE

½ OUNCE FRAGELICO HAZELNUT LIQUEUR

½ OUNCE DARK CRÈME DE CACAO

1 SUGAR CUBE

In a large ceramic or porcelain mug, add ingredients in order and stir well.

COUVET'S ABSINTHE FOUNTAINS

Couvet, Switzerland, the birthplace of absinthe, scores a 9.4 out of 10 on the charm scale. Its residents still appear to be very much rooted in tradition and the rhythms of the seasons. Nearly half of Couvet is farms. The other half is quaint village. On a few mountain paths around town, where locals stop to chat on their way to other business, stand fountains that invariably shelter a few bottles of absinthe left out for public consumption. Those who help themselves will leave a little change next to the bottles in payment. Perhaps they know who put it there to begin with; perhaps they do not. Either way, it's the best kind of open-container rule.

Spiked Hot Chocolate

Hot chocolate. Absinthe. Ski lodge not included.

8 OUNCES HOT CHOCOLATE

1 OUNCE OBSELLO ABSINTHE

Pour hot chocolate into a steamed mug and add absinthe. Top with whipped cream and dust with cinnamon.

Tourment Toddy

The classic hot toddy uses spiced rum, but spiced absinthe opens up a broader range of flavors while retaining the same essential, comforting characteristics.

6 OUNCES BOILING WATER

2 OUNCES LE TOURMENT VERT ABSINTHE

1 TEASPOON HONEY

1 SUGAR CUBE

1 CINNAMON STICK

In a large coffee mug, make as you would a traditional hot toddy. Add the absinthe, honey, cinnamon, sugar, and hot water. Garnish with a lemon wedge.

For a sweeter and spicier brew:

2 OUNCES LE TOURMENT VERT ABSINTHE

2 TABLESPOONS HONEY

1 CINNAMON STICK

1 STAR ANISE

1 CANDIED GINGER

4 WHOLE CLOVES

1 LEMON WEDGE

GEORGE ROWLEY BRINGS ABSINTHE INTO VIRGIN TERRITORY

George Rowley, a suave adventurer, is the Richard Branson of absinthe. Rowley is the force behind La Fée, the first traditional absinthe made in France since the 1915 ban. More important for all of us, the drinkers and the makers, he was largely responsible for parlaying a minor Czech absinthe phenomenon in the 1990s into a worldwide resurgence.

That road began with John Moore, a musician who was traveling through Eastern Europe in 1997 with his band, Black Box Recorder, and wrote about Czech absinthe for an underground London magazine called *The Idler*. The story awakened a dormant curiosity about absinthe and spurred the magazine's publishers to begin exploring ways to import this electric-blue Czech absinthe, Hill's, into the UK. For help navigating the impenetrable bureaucracy surrounding alcohol imports, they called up troubleshooter Rowley, who had succeeded in importing Czech beer into the UK and had worked in commodities and insurance in Prague. Together they formed an importing company called Green Bohemia.

Rowley soon learned that any absinthe Green Bohemia imported would have to pass thirty-six separate chemical tests before being approved for sale in the UK. An exhaustive search turned up three UK labs that could run a combined fourteen of the tests. But how then, you ask, does any outside alcohol ever gain approval in the UK if all the labs put together aren't equipped to administer such tests? The bizarre answer is that no alcohol sold in the UK had ever actually gone through all the tests. Undeterred, Rowley explored outside options and arranged a deal with the University of Prague: the university would perform the tests if Green Bohemia paid for all the chemical reagents they didn't already have available. (As of 2008, the University of Prague is still the only lab in Europe that can do all of the tests required for UK approval.)

Meanwhile, Rowley was hammering out an agreement with the British government that would formalize the legality of importing absinthe. It had never been banned there, but any unusual practice is bound to raise a few eyebrows in London. As Rowley put it, "The reputation seems like . . . something that I've got to be really careful about. So I want to throw the technical book at it." The big barrier was what Rowley terms the "thujone wall," the strict limit of ten parts per million of thujone in any absinthe. Hill's made the cut, but other candidates for import wouldn't. The two parties inked a deal, and by fall 1998, Green Bohemia was making a splash with absinthe in the UK, first at Soho bars and within a year all over the city. By 2000, it had eight brands available, including brands from Spain and Bulgaria.

But Rowley wasn't content with just importing these absinthes. He wanted an authentic French-style absinthe, and the closest anyone had to that in France was the anise-flavored liqueur pastis, which wasn't close enough. Rowley discovered, in a welcome twist on the catch-22—call it a "path-22"—that it wasn't illegal to distill absinthe in France, even though no French distilleries were making it. It was only illegal to *sell* it in France. In the past, distilling in France for export would have made no sense, but with an emerging international market, an authentic, French-made absinthe held real prestige, especially compared with the shock-and-awe absinthes coming out of the Czech Republic.

Now he faced more bewildering challenges than mere British bureaucracy. "The biggest problem with absinthe is, everyone's dead who ever made it. So what do you do?" His answer was to enlist the help of Marie-Claude Delahaye, the preeminent expert on absinthe history and founder of the Absinthe Museum in Auvers sur Oise, France, in re-creating an authentic pre-ban recipe. He worked with a Parisian distillery making pastis to manufacture the French-style absinthe, which he named La Fée and which debuted in 2000.

Selling absinthe has gotten easier over the years. His first customer in London was Johnny Depp, who was in nearby Hertfordshire shooting *Sleepy Hollow* and sent a limo over to get a bottle after reading a newspaper article about it. European Union acceptance in 2001 opened many doors. And finally, when the United States relented in 2007, the floodgates opened. The trade agreement that made it possible was based on the agreement Rowley signed with the British government back in 1998.

Today La Fée is available in twenty countries and comes in three other styles, Absinth Bohemian, X•S Français, and X•S Suisse, but Rowley's emphasis remains authenticity. After every distillation, he says, La Fée couriers a sample to Delahaye for her to taste and approve before he permits the batch to be bottled.

Hard Apple Cider

Obsello is usually thought of as a warm-weather absinthe, but paired with a suite of winter spices, it tastes right at home.

2 OUNCES OBSELLO ABSINTHE

6 OUNCES APPLE CIDER

1 CINNAMON STICK

1 STAR ANISE

1 CLOVE

1 LEMON PEEL

1 ORANGE PEEL

1 SUGAR CUBE

In a large ceramic or porcelain mug, combine ingredients and stir well.

Pomegranate Cider

———

This tart fruit cider, essentially a blend of hot cider and pome-granate juice, is sure to warm when the weather turns harsh.

3 CUPS APPLE CIDER

1 CUP KÜBLER ABSINTHE

½ CUP POMEGRANATE JUICE

2 CINNAMON STICKS

10–15 WHOLE CLOVES

1 ORANGE, SLICED

In a saucepan or Crock-Pot, bring all ingredients to a simmer on low heat. Strain cider into a sugar-rimmed mug. Garnish with an orange twist.

Hot Buttered Absinthe

———

A great party punch for winter holidays; less cloying than the traditional but fatally sweet Hot Buttered Rum.

2 OUNCES ST. GEORGE ABSINTHE

2½ OUNCES APPLE CIDER

1 TABLESPOON UNSALTED BUTTER

1 TABLESPOON BROWN SUGAR

1 CINNAMON STICK

Simmer all ingredients in a saucepan and pour into a steamed mug.

ABSINTHE: GOOD, BETTER, BEST

When the Alcohol and Tobacco Tax and Trade Bureau again permitted distillers to sell absinthe in the United States, it insisted that bottles carry some description other than just "absinthe" in an attempt to prevent brands from trading on the term—in the bureau's words, to avoid naming absinthe as the "class and type designation." Most brands settled on the phrasing *Absinthe Superieure*, which sounds impressive and a bit fanciful, like *Cerveza Mas Fina* on bottles of Corona. But in the pre-ban era, *Superieure* carried a definite, though unofficial, connotation of both quality and percentage of alcohol (about 60 percent). The most desirable term was *Absinthe Suisse*, for absinthes (not only Swiss absinthes) with 65–72 percent alcohol, then *Superieure*, *Absinthe Fine* (55 percent), and *Absinthe Ordinaire* (45 percent). The structure doesn't apply today. Identifying any absinthe as "Suisse" would only lead to confusion, and modern absinthes with alcohol content both high and low use the mid-level *Superieure* name.

Lemon Lick

A lemon herbal tea with a light Swiss absinthe—a nice day-ending drink.

1 OUNCE KÜBLER ABSINTHE

4 OUNCES HOT LEMON HERB TEA, SWEETENED TO TASTE

Pour hot tea and absinthe into mug. Garnish with a lemon wedge.

Hot Punches

Hot Spiced Cranberry

This festive punch is perfect for the large holiday party. St. George and cranberry juice form a tart, strong base tempered by brown sugar and cinnamon.

2 CUPS ST. GEORGE ABSINTHE

4 CUPS CRANBERRY JUICE

2 CUPS APPLE CIDER

¼ CUP BROWN SUGAR

3 CINNAMON STICKS

2 TEASPOONS WHOLE CLOVES

1 LEMON, THINLY SLICED

Simmer all ingredients in a saucepan for about 15 minutes. Let cool slightly and strain into a large bowl. Garnish with a lemon slice and serve warm.

Hot and Hard Apple Cider

Maple syrup brings the spices alive on a cold winter's night.

2 CUPS ST. GEORGE ABSINTHE

8 CUPS APPLE CIDER

¼ CUP MAPLE SYRUP

2 CINNAMON STICKS

2 TEASPOONS WHOLE CLOVES

2 TEASPOONS ALLSPICE BERRIES

1 WHOLE ORANGE PEEL, SLICED

1 WHOLE LEMON PEEL, SLICED

1 WHOLE LEMON, SLICED

Simmer all ingredients, saving one lemon slice for a garnish, in a saucepan for about 15 minutes. Let cool slightly and strain into a large bowl. Garnish with the extra lemon slice and serve warm.

Cold Punches

G.W.'s Cherry Tree

As fruity as a winter punch can get. The cherries are everywhere, but not overly sweet. Though it's technically for winter, as a cold punch, you can get away serving it any time of year. Fourth of July, perhaps?

2½ CUPS ST. GEORGE ABSINTHE

4 OUNCES CHERRY BRANDY

2 PINTS CHERRY SORBET

1 PINT CHERRY PURÉE OR CHERRY JUICE

1 CUP SIMPLE SYRUP

4 CUPS PITTED CHERRIES

Combine all ingredients in a large punch bowl with ice, stir, and serve.

Blood Orange Punch

———

Grand Marnier cuts the tart taste of blood orange juice to create a sweet, dark, exotic party punch.

4 CUPS LUCID ABSINTHE

2 CUPS GRAND MARNIER

4 CUPS BLOOD ORANGE JUICE

1 CUP SWEET AND SOUR MIX

1 CUP GRENADINE

3 BLOOD ORANGES, SLICED AND FROZEN

Thoroughly chill the liquids, combine in a large punch bowl, stir, and serve with sliced oranges.

Cranberry-Apple Punch

———

Lemon-lime ties the whole sparkling package together. A dazzling cold fall punch.

4 CUPS LA FÉE ABSINTH BOHEMIAN

4 CUPS CRANBERRY JUICE

2 CUPS APPLE CIDER

2 CUPS 7UP

2 APPLES, SLICED AND FROZEN

PENNYWISE, POUNDWISE:
THE TRUE COST OF ABSINTHE

A common knock against absinthe is the price, and the sticker shock is understandable if you've never bought it before and expect to pay something akin to the price of a bottle of good wine. But if you measure value in the crudest terms, price per fluid ounce of pure alcohol, the cost of absinthe is quite reasonable. Consider a $69.99 bottle of absinthe with 60 percent alcohol by volume: to buy an equivalent amount of alcohol in a wine (assuming 11.5 percent alcohol by volume), you would have to spend $365.17. Put another way, a mere $13.42 worth of the same absinthe would equal the alcohol in that bottle of wine. Taste and refinement also factor into the equation, of course, but for that you will have to do your own calculations.

Thoroughly chill the liquids, combine in a large punch bowl, stir, and serve with sliced apples.

Winter Punch

Apple is the star here in the form of schnapps, brandy, and garnish. A wonderful winter party punch.

2 CUPS LE TOURMENT VERT ABSINTHE

2 CUPS APPLE BRANDY

2 CUPS SOUR APPLE SCHNAPPS

NOTABLE MOVIES
DEPICTING ABSINTHE

The Affairs of Anatol (1921)
Alfie (1966, 2004)
The Bank Dick (1940)
Blood and Chocolate (2007)
Bram Stoker's Dracula
    (1992)
Bright Young Things (2003)
The Children of the Century
    (1999)
Deceiver (1997)
Fort Saganne (1984)
From Hell (2002)
The Last Samurai (2003)
Lautrec (1998)
Lust for Life (1956)

Madame X (1929, 1937,
    1966)
Manon of the Spring (1986)
Moulin Rouge! (2001)
Murder by Numbers (2002)
My Mother's Castle (1990)
Oscar Wilde (1959)
Pretty Baby (1950, 1978)
Salome's Last Dance (1988)
Time Regained (1999)
Total Eclipse (1995)
Van Gogh (1991)
Van Helsing (2004)
Wilde (1997)
xXx (2002)

2 CUPS CRANBERRY JUICE

1 CUP ROCK CANDY SYRUP

CINNAMON STICKS

Combine all ingredients in a large punch bowl with ice. Slice four apples as floating garnish, stir, and serve.

LOST IN TRANSLATION IN THE SWISS ALPS

Paul Nathan has made a habit of searching out Europe's hallowed absinthe burgs, none more famed than Couvet, the birthplace of absinthe.

Serendipity is a funny thing. I don't speak French, so in Couvet even a task as mundane as asking for sugar in my morning coffee presents a challenge. On my first trip there, a local woman at the next table came to my rescue at the Hotel de l'Aigle, a charming two-hundred-year-old coaching inn at the center of town. After helping me order, she struck up a conversation in English and quickly learned of my search for the origins of the green fairy. "My friend here makes absinthe," she said, gesturing toward a companion at her table as he nudged her to be quiet. "You should come see his still." Had I spoken better French, we would never have met. Serendipity.

Our shared passion for absinthe won out over the man's understandable skepticism, and I soon found myself walking through a storefront, up a flight of stairs, and into a historical apothecary started by his great-grandfather. Amber jars of tinctures and solutions have lined these shelves unchanged for more than a century. This was not a re-creation. It was history frozen in time. Back then, the village apothecary would have sold absinthe from one of these little containers. If he hoped to continue selling it after Switzerland's 1910 ban, he would have had to be cautious indeed.

We descended the stairs and slipped through an herb garden, and my guide swept back an ivy-covered trellis to reveal a closed door that couldn't mask the unmistakable scent of wormwood and anise. Inside stood a beautiful 120-liter-a-day copper still, which he uses to make his Absinthe du Val-de-Travers 55 (smooth and floral, with a hint of pepper). It's en-

tirely legal, but I can only speculate about what might or might not have taken place during the temperate years. Though rumors of clandestine producers from that time abound, an outsider must take care not to ask uncomfortable questions.

Formerly clandestine or not, the tucked-away still, and its results, are magic. And like so much of life, the best things about Couvet involve no ambiguity and require no translation—just an adventurous spirit and a bit of luck.

ACKNOWLEDGMENTS

This project would not have happened without the good faith and backing of our publisher, John Duff, and of our editor, Meg Leder, who crafted a peerless vision for the book without ever drinking any of our absinthe. She was clear-eyed and unflappable throughout, and we are in her debt for it. A big thanks to Brad Crawford for shaping the book and ably bridging the world of absinthe and the world of publishing. Thanks to Ben Gibson for a spirited and evocative jacket design. And thanks to our friend Dave Herlong, who was part chemist, part chef, and part bar historian in creating the supremely good drinks that made our work and this book so worthwhile. Your imagination and attention to detail haven't gone unnoticed. In addition . . .

Paul Nathan thanks: My mother, Pat Nathan, for my love of words. My father, Al Nathan, for my love of life. Barnaby Conrad for introducing my generation to absinthe. My good friend Joegh B. for letting me throw illegal absinthe parties at his place. The California Department of Alcoholic Beverage Control for not throwing the book at me. My lawyer, Paul Spiegel, for getting my absinthe back after the bust (and for keeping me out of jail). The lovely folks of the Vals-de-Travers for being so welcoming and friendly, in particular Gilles Robert, the Val-de-Travers region coordinator for Neuchâtel Tourism. And perhaps most of all, my collaborators for letting me be a part of this wonderful project.

Dave Herlong thanks: George, Gavin, Joe, Phil, and the Maloof family for hosting the biggest party in Las Vegas every night at the Palms Resort & Casino. Michael Morton, Andy Belmonti, Michael Kornick, and the N9NE Group for the honor of letting me work that party! Chef Barry Dakake and the kitchen staff at N9NE Steakhouse for your inspiration, your creativity, and your help in providing the freshest ingredients possible. Sean Cohens for getting me out to that table! Dave Goida, the JOD—John O'Donnell, A.C., Andrea, Tashina, Char, Tommy, Jeremy, Christian, Cheese, Wade, Pat, Trent, Mac, Robbie, and the servers, staff, and management at N9NE for your help and support throughout. You are the best at what you do, and you all inspire me to create and imagine every day. And finally, thank you to my family, George Seyler, Charlotte, David, and Michael Herlong, for your love and support.

INDEX

ABOUT THE AUTHORS

Paul Owens discovered absinthe while traveling through Europe in the mid-1990s. Years later, at his San Francisco bar, the Fish Bowl, the staff would occasionally break out samples of European absinthe for regulars, a ritual Paul embraced even before meeting his law-flouting co-author in 2005 at one of the latter's well-known absinthe-tasting parties. Paul's restaurant, Tortilla Heights, features two popular absinthe cocktails, the Mexican Wrestler and the Deep End.

Paul Nathan's absinthe adventures began after running with the bulls in Pamplona, Spain, which led to smuggling home Spanish absinthe, which led to absinthe-tasting parties in San Francisco. In 2006, agents from the California Department of Alcoholic Beverage Control and local police raided one of his absinthe parties. To this day, Paul and his bartenders remain the only people arrested for selling absinthe during America's ninety-five-year ban. His explorations have taken him to private absinthe collections, bootleg stills, wormwood farms in the Swiss Alps, and absinthe distilleries throughout

Europe. When not traveling as a professional magician, Paul writes for Absintheparty.com and throws decadent parties.

ABOUT THE MIXOLOGIST

Award-winning mixologist **Dave Herlong**, the mastermind behind the book's contemporary cocktail recipes, develops the specialty cocktails and drink lists for all the venues at the Palms Resort & Casino in Las Vegas: N9NE Steakhouse, Rain, Ghostbar, Moon Nightclub, the Playboy Club, and the Palms Pool & Bungalows. He has created the official drink list for the Sundance Film Festival, and his cocktails have appeared in newspapers, magazines, TV shows, and the hands of countless celebrities in search of refreshment.